WE'LL SEE WHO SEDUCES WHOM

a graphic ekphrasis
in verse

visuals: David Aronson
verbals: Tom Bradley

Unlikely Books
www.UnlikelyStories.org
P. O. Box 2794
Lafayette, LA 70502

We'll See Who Seduces Whom
Visual Art Copyright © David Aronson 2013
Text Copyright © Tom Bradley 2013
Book and Cover Design Copyright © Tom Bradley and Unlikely Books, 2013

All Rights Reserved

ISBN-13: 978-0-9708750-7-5

The Library of Congress has issued this edition
a Control Number of 2013949110

Unlikely Books
www.UnlikelyStories.org
New Orleans, Louisiana

Everything possible to be believed is an image of truth.
—William Blake

CANTO I.

Whose head is given here, whose gotten?

My hair's good now. Strands flow along my head in triple time. This is topmost, as it conducts objective love.

So, little man. You've gotten yourself into a pretty predicament. Can you be surprised by your leeching? Someone must have chanted you the caution:

> Jaw parasites!
> Speech feeders, they fasten!

You didn't hear the teaching?

Photon tubes are native to these parts. They generate in litters of three when vapor descends to rub certain fronds. The static charge incubates stiff wormlets, which move outward and triangulate upon the oblivious, the self-involved, the brain-wrapped. Slow drill rape of phonemes commences.

In case you weren't paying attention, I'll whisper you the hymn again:

> Word thieves, they fasten!
> Antiparticulate drainers of the lower mandible!
>
> If lightning rods shit elementary bosons,
> these shiny cylinders ionize thought-flatus!
>
> Cathodes, catheters!
> Famished face fornicators!
>
> They fasten! They fasten!

Haven't you an ear to listen?

I do. Please note how nicely mine is deployed under my hairdo, which remains unmussed, despite all this plasmatical fuss. Thanks are due to my barrette of burnished onyx, black and igneous, just like you.

See it topside? Upper-left corner? Foursquare in cross-section, it's as good an anchor as I'll need, and as firm a context. This proud bauble of mine's the sort of solid geometry a regular child would want penetrating her darling noggin.

You're nailed tolerably well yourself, friend.

Know what let's do? If you mock the Passion of the Triply Transfixed, I'll agree to feign three Marys' worth of astonishment.

Okay? Fun? Yes?

Can you hear me?

Oh, sorry. Of course you can't. A little man so fixed on his own raw brain as to disdain all means of locomotion—why would he bother to grow inlets for speech?

> Your trio of malnourished talk-suckers
> milk a vacuum that throbs like a migraine.
>
> No ears, no music, no hair.
> Neither love, objective nor sub-,
> nor particular Passion to mock.
>
> Just sit on your rock.
> Try not to roll off.

And concentrate on wrenching that voluptuous grunt of effort from your lips.

Such flexing nostrils! Big work is getting done inside you, I can tell. Cerebral bowels are in motion. Witness your exhaust manifold and the tiny ecosystem it suckles.

Eyeless albino slugs are known to graze around magma vents in ocean trenches.
Should I, then, open wide and inhale your burnt syllables, my small obsidian hookah?

    Should I counter-metamorphose
    to a three-inch caterpillar
    and fellate your pretty pipe stem,
    lovely, larvally,
    while, from the corner of my nursing maxillae,
    demanding of any brunette-coiffured girls
    who happen to tiptoe near,
    "You! Who are you?
    (And why did you dye so dark?)"

    Yes, I should. I want to know who.
    My virgin jaw drops to accommodate you.

Just so.
Oh, by the way. I won't laugh,
little man. Probably. But what will it
matter? Who'll know? Few come
into these woods,
whatever sound I make,
or face I pull,
or words I thieve to tell
a borrowed joke.
There'll be no need
for a post-coital smoke.

Okie-doke. Here goes.
Suck in, retain. Swallow, as it were.
Wait a tiny while...

Oh, my.

My dark hors d'oeuvre, my Baptist,
brought to me on a rough platter!

Whose head is given here?
Whose gotten?

We'll See Who Seduces Whom.

CANTO II.

**Unprepuced Yahweh, Sovereign of Scrotal Sinai!
Conjoined Asherah, Twin of Parasitic Concubinage!**

Whom I took for little man,
toked as water pipe and ridiculed
as navel-gazer short one torso,
flung that shortage in my face
two, three times, and turned into—

—The Fire Pillar!

Who hunches forward!
Who snouts into all see-holes!
From whose soul-chagrining gaze
all profane eyes recoil!

I'm left limp to recapitulate the best I can. Let's see. Where was I?

Where mist, not lava, cascades down
to fecundate, not fricassee,
I think I might recall—

Yes, I teased a tiny Negro, by a fall
that, no doubt, shares a figurative source
with this luxuriant basting sauce
of licked and refluxed amniotic caul.

The toy grub primps
the snapping turtle's tongue.
He was such a lure,
a shaken darling tastebud.

My girlish whim was to approach
his Hamite head obliquely.
That left-hand coyness was my flair,
flippancy my error, when,
puffed with cheek and pretty hair,
I curtsied round to condescend.

You maintained your oral flexure, your flaring nares, your aspect of psychic stool-straining. But when I minced into full frontality, you gigantized, little man.

Negro, you brightened. Your earless skull grew colored skin that gorged us both. You rolled back rock eyelids, glared, and candled what hatches, hidden, under planetary crust:

> Stiff wormlets I glimpsed,
> once fully apprehended,
> shed cylindricality
> and sinewed into throats,
> pumping down to one person, triplicate.
>
> Skin-deep leeches nibbling words
> merely emblematized,
> to my undeflowered eyes,
> triumvirs knotted, chomping.
>
> Photonic gizmos snapped
> a shadow polaroid,
> resolved upon my retinae
> only post-epiphanically:
>
> The Holy Hungry Family's
> subsoil picnic tug-o'-war!

This is not the Passion, partner, we bargained for. Just pulled into the second station, yet already time to cry with a loud voice and give up the ghost.

You might say I blew it.

> Unprepuced Yahweh,
> Sovereign of Scrotal Sinai!
> Conjoined Asherah,
> Twin of Parasitic Concubinage!
> Hear you both my inbred supplication:

Won't you say it isn't me,
unfeignedly astonished,
unhaired, chastised, scarlet vomit-baptized,
who bawls propitiation, supine
in your plural Hindu arms?

Have we seen, now, who seduces whom?
If our creche be a death wrestle,
Mother/Auntie, I'm in trouble
with that heavy priestess-butcher's
thumb of yours.

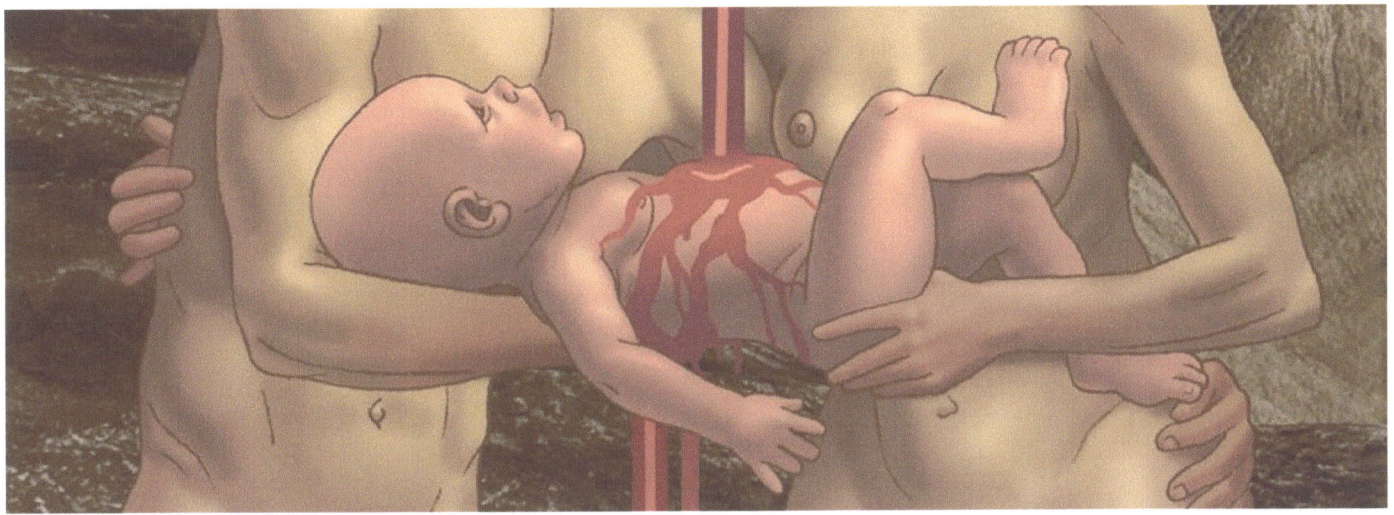

Solomon proposed adjudicating parental identity by dividing the spoil like a wish bone—

—but, wait. Hold on.

What does Baby see, way high?
What uneasy noggin lies
and wears the molten asphaltous tiara,
triple, of this Pyroclasmic Pope?
What upper seismic whiteness spreads
to show me hope?

Lush suede though this coat we share may be,

    there's a certain epidermal dearth
    along the spousal siblings' scalp.

The hero for whom vulnerability's named also
presents with compromised connective tissue—but
at the other end of his doomed, dipped corpus.
Your godhead's botched topside, Pops.

    Baby sees something brittle.
    And it isn't burnished onyx.
    For all our mutual hextupality,
    you've not been fully hatched.

    Like Julius and Ethel's Jello box,
    your line is dotted, folks,
    your time allotted.

    So I will sulk in my red vest
    and keep an eye fixed on unfleshed
    seams where parents' head bones mesh.

    Was that Negro you, Papa?
    And is your craw the source
    of hemorrhage that swaddles Junior?

    The Child who chokes migrainous unions
    incubates divorce.

WE'LL SEE WHO SEDUCES WHOM.

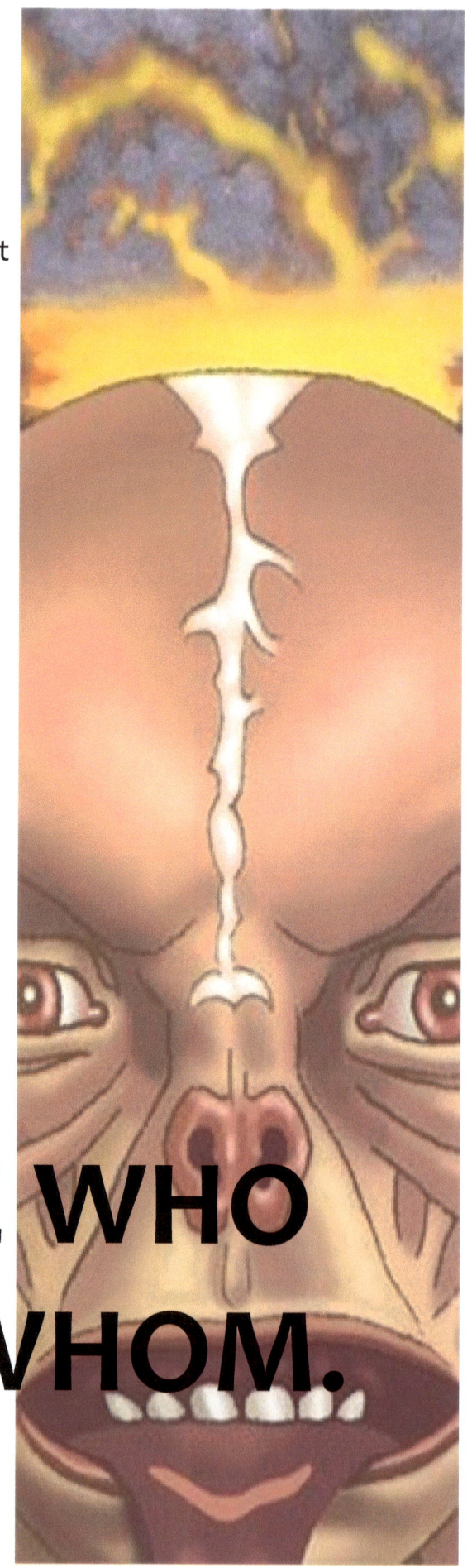

CANTO III.

**If this Megalo-Mestiza Mamacita be me,
who remains for you to be?**

Whose lower extremity's fixing to plunge
deep as both throats of schizoform Pluto?

Whose shiny prosthesis unhymens this prairie,
obtruding on soil like a smooth hookah-tube
urged on a flippant girl, trying to get her to
do smoke as vulvas do semen?

Quick as aroma can conjure remembrance,
she breathes and conceives a volcanic cavern
not far underfoot, where rain never runs,
nor hominid squads with musical outlets,
but rock surely flows, runny as barf
from bifurcate gullets of morfadyke godlets
bathing their bastard.

It's a pipe. It's a lingam. It's Archangel
Michael's electrical Earth-acupuncturing
needle, now poised to get mainlined
with more than sufficient avoirdupois
to ground it home—like which there's no place.
(Repeat that with three clicks of mineralized footwear.)

And, speaking of which, we've officially flitted
from Garden to Sheol and up to lapsarian Kansas,
where Caucasoid children in period garments
and cereal deserts come standard issue—
lightning rods, also, for rumbling reasons.

Around these parts, the latter paraphernalia are misconstrued, after the colloquial fashion, to be high-ampere plasma attractors. In vernacular they're termed stiff wormlets, or tubular photon leeches, and are quaintly claimed to drain inclement speech off these uncannily hovering cumulonimbi.

The bolts of patois such throats
    gulp from our vault:
"I want a divorce," and
    "That's spousal assault."

("As above so below,"
    lisps Philo Judaeus,
mildly seconding
    H. Trismegistos,
who flinches behind
    a fastidious wrist.)

    Macro- and micro-
meteorologically speaking,
upstairs is a little man's
    prognathous chin.
Negroid, gargantuan,
    from our vantage point,
he's letting himself be
    phonetically face-raped
by mentalized supercells,
    such as the doozy
mesocyclone that threatens
    to leech our quartet
of sentient beings away.

If, somehow, already, you've mustered the strength, feel free to upgrade it to a quintet. I'll be right behind you. Maybe.

Meantime, it's okay to wax colloquial. We're beyond climatology, anyway. For example, in local sodbuster lore—

The lightning is a yellow schwanz
which urethrizes prostate rain,
spermatizing nitrogen,
soixante-neufing oxygen,
in fixation that's said to frame
emotional, not atmospheric wants.

Wherever a catastrophic discharge of such Spooge Elemental chooses to zap its motile electrons, seedlings and sprouts get jump-started—or so they say—along with the glorified breakfast grass natives esteem toasted (currently stabbed and trampled as stubble underfoot), plus every regional species of squirmer, writher, mewler, puker—

—each of which, for your edification, I now propose to marshal in broad, generous panoramical parade (outsized mutations unnaturally deselected):

Grasshoppers, corn-borers, crow jokers,
milk-reeky litters of barnyard paramours
that crouch on all fours, crotch-level
Future Farmers of Where-the-Hell-Ever
who, before acquiescing to lifetime interment
in wheatmeal silos, take trumpet lessons
for expression of ostensible inner selves,
or, lacking talent, become percussionists.

All thanks to the Omni-Begetting Cycle Biogeochemical, and our rural-free-delivery system thereof:

The overburdened peg leg here depicted.

Lynchpin, Fixator of Love Objective, see it? This item can be pinpointed, not to say isolated, among sundry size-four sneakers, way down in the lower portion of the frame (where you are urged, for your own safety, to huddle and shelter your see-holes till I sound the all-clear).

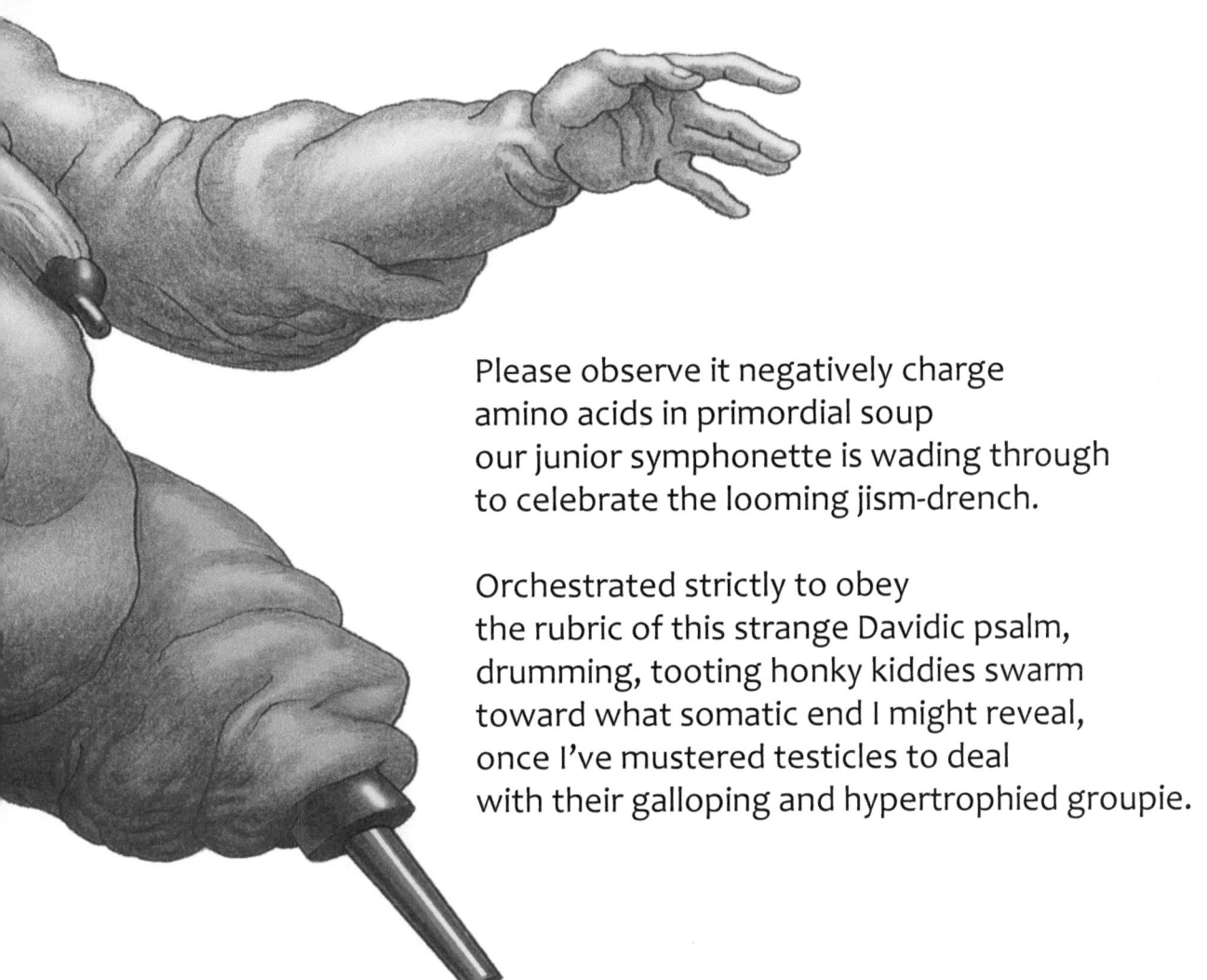

Please observe it negatively charge
amino acids in primordial soup
our junior symphonette is wading through
to celebrate the looming jism-drench.

Orchestrated strictly to obey
the rubric of this strange Davidic psalm,
drumming, tooting honky kiddies swarm
toward what somatic end I might reveal,
once I've mustered testicles to deal
with their galloping and hypertrophied groupie.

I just lost my train of thought. Where was I?

* * * *

Forgive me for losing track so soon. As you surely noticed long ago, I'm not being confronted by such sights as conduce to orderly ekphrasis. And ekphrasis is the task at hand—admittedly self-imposed. (Nobody else has offered to pitch in.)

> Was I just hoarsely hymning
> litho-atmo-hydro-bio-noospherics
> to petrify, to blow away,
> to rinse off, overgrow, unthink
> what I'd rather not own up to?

I'm no would-be Tantric initiate dork seeking to transgress the granny-gag reflex by wallowing nostril-deep in climacteric bloat. Yet, how willingly the see-hole's raw orifice–

–takes in her skin,
and her children's skins,
and how their silver steam's
untethered to surface area,
untroubled by surface tension,
unaware of the surface
that's somehow been caused
not to exist,
upon which they're rendered–
if rendered they be,
and not marching a triumph
in untenseful time
immeasurable to the mere
grammar-mired likes of me.

Have I with flippancy been masking three Marys' worth of unfeigned astonishment?

    Do I deny abject, prostrate awe
    of the Elemental Being
    my eyeballs are now seeing—
    rather, emphatically are not?

Yet again I've lost my train of thought.

In a landscape where the very terms of bodily configuration must be dickered and bartered with odd-sized indigenoids, where personhood herself can be sapped any second–

> –where a 'tween can get squeezed in an infantile frame
> and a solo noggin sprouts two bods in a blink–

–one particular type of item is needed.

By its very straight-edged configuration this specific thing sheds directionality on the chaos that impends in each oblique slant of our shifty neighborhood light.

Could you kindly scan the lower reaches of this world and pitch in?

Spot me an impersonal bearings-getter, a serviceable object, reasonably inanimate. Make sure it retains sharp highlights in the indirect gloom that presages strange twisters. That's the dead giveaway.

> Unearth me a geometry-conduit,
> the isolatable kind, manufactured,
> not incubated, orgasmed or shat.

> It clicks like an instrument at flip of thumbnail,
> and won't be gooshed in fistfuls of sebaceous misgivings
> no matter how squeezed in mud-drowned panic.

Under our ceiling of blown murk, I must ask you to keep an eye peeled for squared-away sheen that recalls stone's cool infertilities–

—not bare-naked billows
of unabashed birthday suit,
unhemmed as hashish smog
burped from a hookah stem,
unsculpted of paleo-mud
that never felt kiln,
viral, fecal,
gooshy by temperament
with degenerate nephric duct:
the mammoth in the unwalled room.

Until bearings are gotten (if available to be got),
we must ignore a certain jiggling backdrop.
Pay no attention to the thing behind the
meat-curtain.

Above all, in the knotted bowels of Christ,
call it by no name.

> Nothing's there,
> draped in pendant pleats,
> convoluted as weather,
> hung with funnels,
> down-sucked twisters,
> a nightmare pair.
>
> Spread-eagled, God help us,
> nearly coextensive with the planetary brink.
>
> What mustn't Baby see, or think?
>
> Like Unprepuced Yahweh
> Sovereign of Scrotal Sinai's
> soul-chagrining, eye-recoiling gaze,
> it can't be borne by mortal retinae—

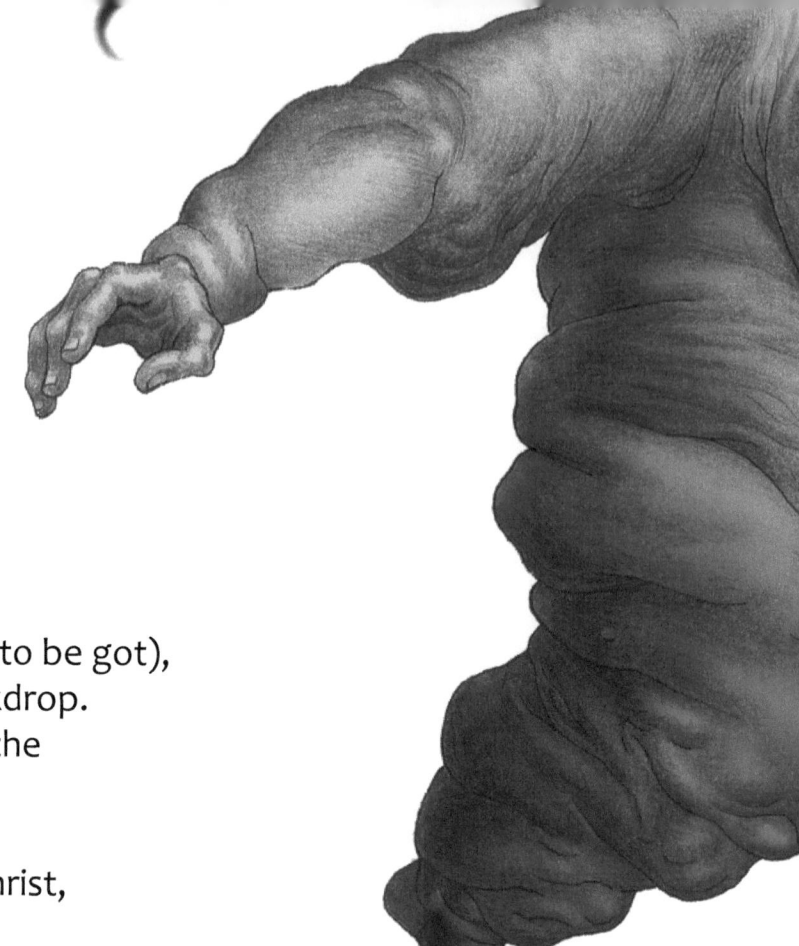

How a painter gets perfect light,
inhuman, supernal, on a galumphing gimp.

How a poet in thought-raping beauty
with dactyls consecrates sarcasm.

How players in the league of four-armed deities
beguile a quadrillion-year midmorning's lassitude
with Creation, then a yawn or two,
then Dissolution Universal, impromptu.

Here is no ickiness, no prettiness,
no piety, no depravity. Just undulation.

All you may say of Unthinkable That
is something seems to be breathing.

An altered extension of the sub-atom's enharmony
for no excuse beyond the flimsiest: being.

Whole planets tambourined like toys,
spat-valved from tin horns by pointless boys
dancing catastrophe in nature's umbrage,
itself gone at first smoky blink of Kansoid light—

—left-handed twister harbinger,
photonic filigree-tracer
of myriad reverend stretch marks,
satin-silvery, inevitable, beaut—

—mom of God. Where did that come from?

No one has seen the Face of Guess-Whom
and lived. Nor the knockers, I presume,
not merely unbecoming, but undoing.

"How 'bout the nether parts?"
pants horny Moses through a wet beard.
"I mean, in a pinch, heh-heh?"

Volcano Slum Lord Jehovah!
Shield our see-holes from cauterization
by the sheer aspect
of these particular Nethers.

Send us Your Child, sweet
brunette Daughter/Niece,
perfect phiz upturned.
Strategically place her,
blameless, in annihilating light.

Make her a Mary if you insist.
Shoe her in junior-miss Mary Janes,
though the ground she prances be holy,
unbush her pre-pubed nether parts,
in this place of mowed bristle.

She'll be our bush, bright face
unconsumed by ignition that crackles
the ambient element, her maracas
Elijah's still, small vocal testicles.

Horizon dead-level,
her sight-line's a signal
to rise no further.

I won't. You shouldn't, either.

WE'LL SEE WHO SEDUCES WHOM.

CANTO IV.

**Black Virgin, Smelter-Nigredo,
Hammered of Yard Steel,
Hot from Gdansk!**

Downcasting my see-holes in doubled woe,
appalled, I'd settle for just one pebble
on this harrowed plain, to stub a single toe.

Give me a rock, one, preferably stout-hearted,
and I'll soon show you the Cham refuting Berkeley.

Or, dark with celestial iron,
something rendered immaculate
of astrobacteriology will do,
unpanspermatozooic, precipitated
from the alternative vault.

I'd downright embrace
Multi-Dugged Artemis,
Diorite Artifice of Ephesus
cum-Black Virgin, hot from Gdansk,
Iconical Polackess hammered of yard steel,
neither gravid, imaginative, nor milked.

I hereby submit to invoke
Smelter Madonna, the Tidied
Antibacterial Pseudo-Nigredo
of certified Popish endorsement.

At least the latter, swart as a bad dream though she be, comes modestly draped, unlike the hefty hussy whom I invite you now to circumlocute in fastidious panic with me, till her epiphany. Inevitable and black as a Kansoid thunderstorm, it will feel like undead burial in a silica sand box of fulgurite tubes, fused subsurface.

Till that terrible time—

    —the Family's unholy tug-o'-war
    yet being unbrought to issue,
    slow drill-rape of inwards continues.

****

Carpocratian Christ, time gone by,
displayed a split-level aspect:
divine, degenerate or nebbishly neither—

—depending on the beholder's state of soul-preparedness.

    Likewise, to the vulgarian's gawk,
    from the right knee up, we've got a ringer
    for Gaia Whoozit's kitschier depictions.

Hobbled by man's inhumanity to subhumanity,
conducting her cubs' rudimentary lament

for Nature abused, she is the Mundane—
in yawning, as opposed to serpentine mode.

Trendily hurt as by a trite spouse,
her non-foot's a weepy handicap,
rather than tantalization
sharp from the Realm of Ideals.

Boilerplate Slinger of Mismatched Curd Bags!
Straddler of Quim Unpeekabootiable!
Command from us, your cunt-kisser canaille,
unexamined life-reverence—by reflex, yet!

    Kaboodle-clangor, clatter of kit
    bestow upon our cerumen pits!
    Should we forget our Mammy's praise
    rock itself would grunt and shit!

    Missing toes of your own to tap,
    you decree all should remain prostrate
    for a season of hyper-percussification
    so that, vanity pulled down by monotony,
    selves rendered numb and suggestible,
    linear shwanzes be shed,
    and all centaur-ants should sway,
    clitoral, catamenical, tribal.

This is an especial requisite for pre-dead white phallus packers, such as our parade
marshal, the unfeathered peacock up front.

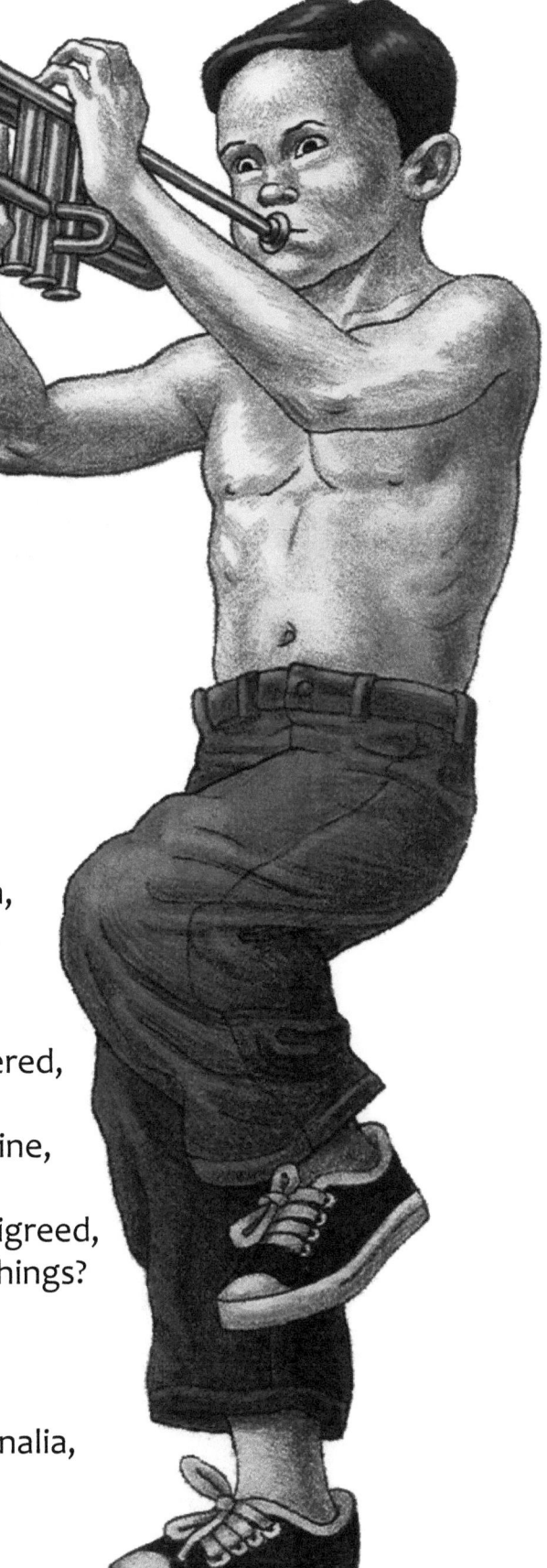

Bonering up that unslid trombone
like some priapic Elohist orthodoxy?
Forty five degrees? How dare he?

See and condemn him!
Flaunting with smugness
his unearned privilege!
Preceding Ma herself!

Damn this brat
upside his pea-pod prostate
three times!

Holistically hex him, unsex him,
his presumptuous nephric duct,
his unshirted ne'er-drooper nenes!

Is this kid, or calf, or suckling
piglet prepped for the surprise
bash that hovers over his head,
the ham-fisted neck snapper?

It's he and none other who's kept
Carnality's Consecrated Curtain drawn,
lo, all these drab multi-millennia, tight
on the Age of Unbrassiered Isis!

Why shouldn't Mom's bust go unhaltered,
netted around as it's been
with voluptuous puckers, crepe de Chine,
crinkled in ribbons of nacreous sheen
tat for teats, enlaced, embosomed, filigreed,
crocheting its own selves' exo-underthings?

Realer than living latex, tucked
in a drawer of big lady powder puffs,
eyelash curlers, thigh garter paraphernalia,
and—

—mom of God's son in execution-swaddle. I don't even want to guess where that one came from.

Quick, where's a stiff straw to grasp at?
Something to squeeze—
Do I recall soliciting aid of some sort?

Were we (you and I, that is) scoping out the serviceable getter of bearings, the item that might be glimpsed poking around here—

The Conduit Geometrical?

If so, friend—how can I put it nicely? The ear-hole besiegers being swung in our faces aren't what I have in mind.

Cones, cylinders, ovoids, disks unbiased as per The Forms Platonic—

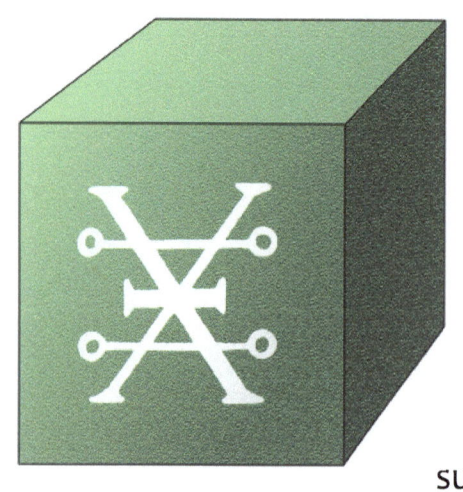

—their basic structural components are presentable enough.
No organic outlines mucking around there.
But they come so elaborated with spit-valves, of all things, and such jangly rim cymballettes

as Euclid never delineated, nor ever got pilfered off Pythagoras—rather more likely tinkered by Sousa and his tin-eared ilk—plus head-tightener wing nuts and strap-on fist grips, not to mention—

—that up-front honker
　　with the tinselly lacquer,
　　self-involved in reflex coils
　　like some feathered reptilian,
　　Nilic, Aztec or Punjabberwockish,
　　dorking and gobbling in self-simultaneity.

By all means, let us have something shiny as brass leading the way—

The Wilderness Pillar

　　　　　　—but could we unkink the tired old Ouroboros, just
　　　　　　a smidgen? Ergonomics can be laid gently aside,
　　　　　　twisted as we already are, tangled as we've
　　　　　　become, and have been—

　　　　　　　　-since our precipitous dip
　　　　　　　　 to the Rim Rhadamanthic
　　　　　　　　one panel back, or so,
　　　　　　　　 in our Cosmogonical Triptych,
　　　　　　　　　multiple worlds ago,
　　　　　　　　　 when time was yet untenseful,
　　　　　　　　　and skin, where it obtained,
　　　　　　　　　 was taut yet unstretched,
　　　　　　　　and "to sag" was a concept,
　　　　　　　　 like Plato's doodads or shirtless lads,
　　　　　　　　　that needed no immediate fucking with—

　　　　　　　　—where unitary execs pouted
　　　　　　　　 like obsidian gravel on stone superficies,
　　　　　　　　　unprepossessing as black apples of eyes,
　　　　　　　　　 and juvenile demi-vierge Eves
　　　　　　　　　　could put out for free, confident
　　　　　　　　(if falsely) of no deep involvement.

Back then I had something going for me. I miss my pretty accessory.

> Burnished onyx, it anchored,
> solidified context and fixed
> a girl's darling noggin
> on matters at hand,
> like underpinned dactyls,
> but silently, no back-up band.

We could stand a little bobby-pinning right about now.

> Fasten our think-hanks,
> comb out brain-cockleburs,
> deploy notions in parallel
> strands of triple time signatures.
> Hairs unruly in snags exacerbate
> splitting migraines with jagged parts.

Where has that serviceable bauble gone off to?
Again I ask you to pitch in and poke around.

> In our dangerous neighborhood
> the rapists are tutelary godlets
> who forcibly fob attributes.
>
> I've played the hash-hazed caterpillar
> to your pebble with a wince, or
> your eight-limbed godhead, or not.
>
> An undiapered primitive baby, bloody?
> Says who? I know I am, but what are you?
> Rubber, glue? Protoplasm?

It's not unreasonable to expect hair ornaments to join the fray, to assume sentience and commence behaving. Do you see a burrow for a shiny black mole?

Of course, around here, when you hear words like "mole" and "burrow," the last place to look is down. Maybe the identity tag, the species marker, the signal, is placed with uncharacteristic logic on high, like beacons in normalcy, and the clue is topside.

So it's okay to glance up, beyond the sky-scraping solar plexus that has heretofore been our horizon—but only if you pledge, on pain of petrification, to hear my caution:

This may be a death wrestle
in some breadbasket Peniel,
but you're no Jacob (so far)
and I see no spandexed angel—

—so you'd better make like Aaron's
mush-mouthed baby brother
and flinch from the—

Visage Unviewable!

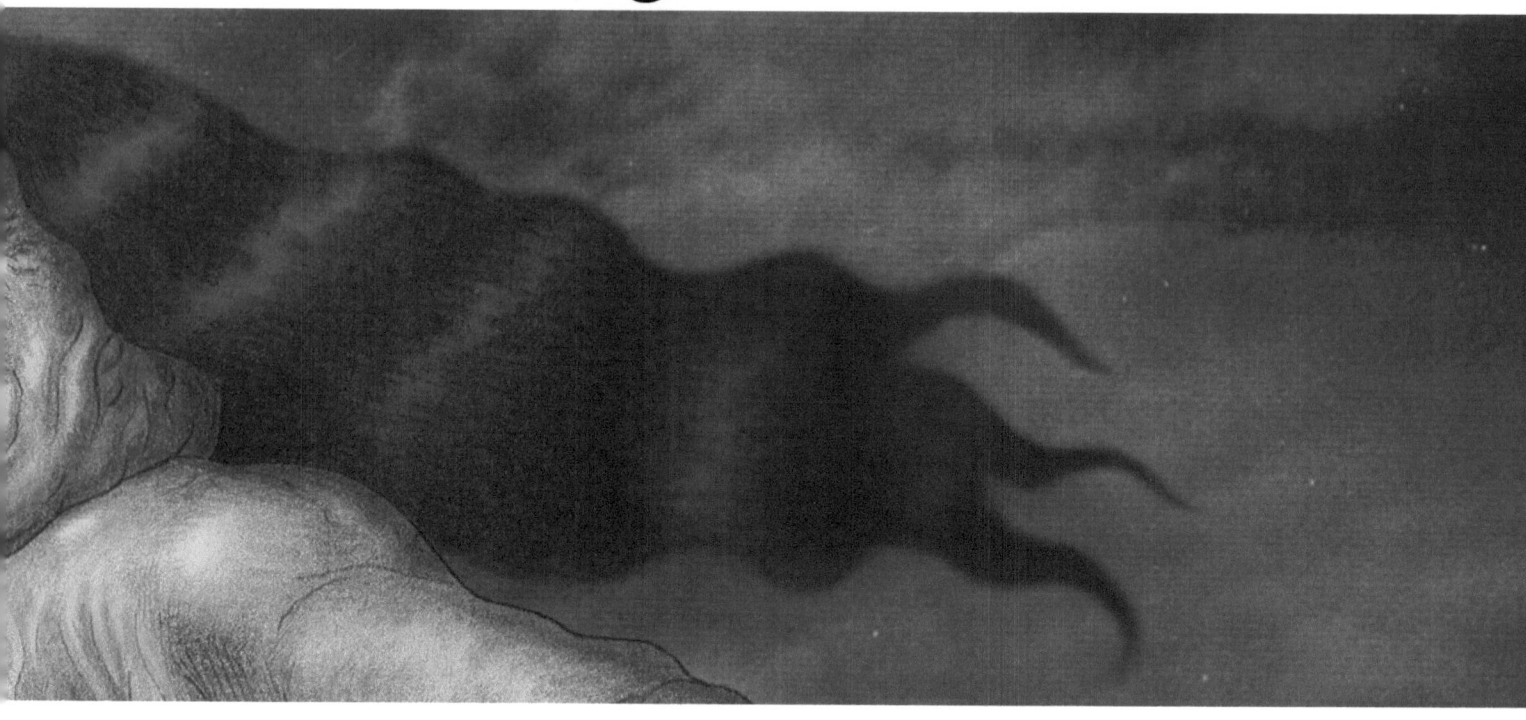

Skip ahead. The head.
See only sable tresses, and refrain
from expecting to hear named
the owner of the corrugated scalp
from which they so ideally issue.

Though, by way of paradox,
they trail in a pre-twister gale
which, to all superficial
appearances, has blown away—

The Fastener Desiderated

—this luxuriant mane remains unmussed,
the Ideal of the Marcel Style
scotch-taped on the mirror
of The Beautician Immaterial—

—the sole immobile element in our Composition Elemental, even as, in contradiction that can only obtain in parts like these—

—it flows in triple time,
conducts objective love.

Such a classicized coif constitutes its own barrette, as it were, almost identifying the impermissibility beneath as—
—no, not yet.

Don't look topside. I changed my mind. Please focus your gaze back down upon the unfruited plain. Retract, again, like a ping-ponged testicle, or four, with apologies for my undulant cowardice.

If you knew what was coming, you'd cover your nether parts, too, with both hands—if not more.
* * * *

Help me look for a different shape: not cuboid, but circular in cross-section, in the style of the Logo Universal—I mean the other, anti-yonic one, longer than wide.

We'll make it a game. That should be diverting. Okay? Fun? I'll throw you a subtle riddle-hint, a reminder:

    It's a stick. It's a dick. It's hot, and a rod.

Except in color, it resembles a gam
contrived of jaw-ivory, about to slam
its glamorous pivot in the poopdeck
of this dry-docked Pequod—

—as though, with all our trouble
we've not been denying Kybele
or Hathor or who-the-Hecate
ever, but rather the latter tub's
dead-reckoning chief exec.

Shod like that hop-jump-skipper,
yet built like his nemesis,
gimpery aside, considering the flipper,
she's got the full-figured beauty,
instead, to pull sea monster duty.

Is the famed pair tangled here, just as dear
Herman left them? Think of the children—

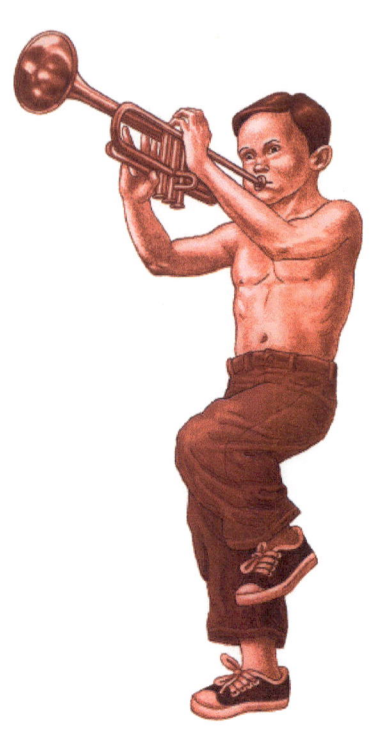

Like latent nancies harpoon-boating
nuts-to-butts, yet yearning
with their persons to ballast
the Mother Ship's nethers
(where they get to squeeze sperm),
do the youngsters slosh athwart
a Leviathan monocephalically mingled
with Jezebel's hubby's namesake—

(call me fish-smell)

—not unlike somebody—rather, bodies—
whom we've—rather, I've—already met
and sweet-talked downstairs:
that marital mismatch,
mutually self-harassed
to the ends of the planet
their inter-wadded selves encompass?

If the erstwhile creche was a death-wrestle,
do we see a rematch in full grapple?

That's indecorous.
I'll bawl in your arms
but not share your skin—

—though this one has the capacity. If it didn't before, it's been stretched.

What jiggles in my face is perhaps not ethnic cellulite after all, but brine blubber. So where is the whiteness that above all should appall us? Shouldn't she be parmacetically-pale?

Darkness can clue,
one supposes, hue
being less relative than size,
to our weird neighborhood eyes.

Nearly black as the first little pebble
that tried not to roll off undressed stone
in our initial Eden, also leeched three times,
she's neither Alice nor Dorothy nor Moby, but—

—Megalo-Mestiza Mama!

There, I named her. Now she's to be dealt with. No way around it.
If I may take a moment to get personal—

Which bits of Triple-M display the highest melanin content, lending the coloration
of, say, certain forms of igneous rock? And which elements of her sacrosanct person
most strongly resemble, in general configuration as well as pristine surface texture,
our previous manifestations of that volcanic material?

You shouldn't have to peer too far or hard to spy an answer. With the exception of the bits under inquiry, this creature seems committed to rugosity as a way of being—

>—from scalp to left toes
>(the ones that are left)
>not sleek cetaceousness,
>but Pachydermy Personified.

>Even her eyeballs—which, in other creatures
>except for chameleons and LSD eaters
>are not overburdened with nubbles,
>lid-snagging ridges or lash-tanglers–
>have abandoned their sockets
>rather than see, and be seen, unpuckered.

As a matter of fact—

>>Apart from the prosthesis,
>>her only non-ridgy bits
>>are the tips of the tits.

>>**Note how stylized,**
>>**in configuration purified,**
>>**one could say geometrized–**
>>**oddly, in this withered context,**
>>**given obsidian luster,**
>>**or sheen of onyx.**
>>
>>**At long last! Have we found—**

Our Conduit Geometrical

—in multiple form, yet?

In a place like this, since everything else is up for grabs (if "up" could signify in such an Arsy-Versyville), we take the few laws we do manage to enact quite seriously. Revealed scripture, that sort of thing.

Back down in Luridity's Lair, where spawn are christened in amniotic retch, equipment violations may get played fast and loose with; but here—

> It's been decreed
> that tubes should leech
> compliant with local liturgy,
> and, like thrills or troubles,
> come in threes.

License is granted
to litters so numbered
when vapor—or, as here,
a torrent in buckets, in tubs—
descends to rub fronds,
or ravage scythed grain-stubs.

Ergo, her nips are tacked, not intrinsic.
They recapitulate the parallel prop or pivot
below, whose identical cylindrical sheen
its upper two siblings share,
as if to reflect their sheer
mutual significance.

Constellation-girding, a thousand-
minus-997 points of etcetera
in the epidermal dark:
Orion's Grandmammy's truss.

Trebled tubelets emit Clear Bardo Light!
And I don't mean Bridgette, though it is a small span
from somewhere to nothingness,
and possibly back again—
so saith The Book of the Pre-Maoist Dead.

Is she equipped or beset
with photonic suckers of phonemes?
Is this a prelingual pun
or (impossible thought)
do identities blur here
promiscuously as carcasses
in one reified scum called skin?

Juxtapose the former Tiny Negro
with Melanical Monstro-Mother.
Lay one transparency over the other,
and I guarantee
you will see
congruent isosceles.

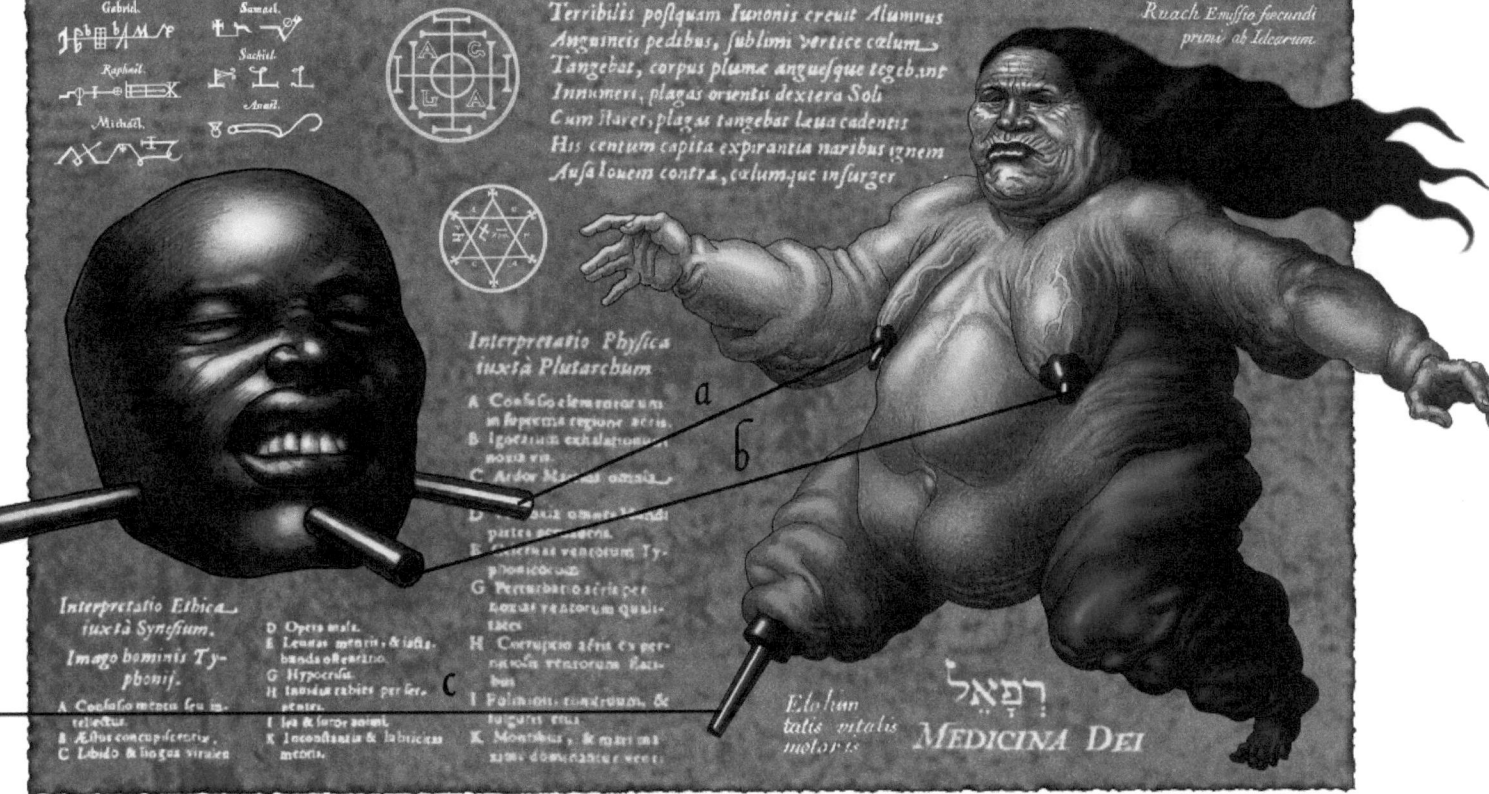

Does this torso, in some protean way,
resemble a pinioned, parasite-ridden jaw
whose owner, taunted as limbless long ago,
now is only twenty-five percent so?

Has the question been sufficiently begged yet?
Who the hell is this darksome witch–
or should I say not who, but which—

—the integrity, even existence, of whose skeletomusculature can only be surmised?

Being subjected to treble transfixity in a mocking manner, is she? Does that sound familiar?

Has a bargain been kept?
If so, who's keeping?
And with whom?

Is she,
from one point of view—

—you?

Little man, have you gotten yourself into a predicament? Is it pretty?

WILL WE SEE SOME SEDUCING SOON?

CANTO V.

**There's a very loud amusement park right in front of my present lodgings.
—Nabokov, *Pale Fire***

Does it feel as though the Many Tentacled Vulva is stalking you through ankle-deep lactose excreted from geometrically-nippled black-widow teats?

Not only are the tubes recapitulated, but the breasts from which they protruded in their last manifestation. And the means with which these paired lightning rods fructify the planet underfoot has condensed from high-ampere plasma to arachnid milk.

Does it seem as though you are being prick-teased by a child who likes to feign fellatio on geometrical solids, meanwhile wearing a facial expression sultry beyond her years, as estimated by an examination of such segments of her toothsomely chubby torso as are currently oglable by the salacious eye?

Are you sad because the band has broken up, your trumpet confiscated and replaced by this slut's piccolo—not horn, but pipe? She has more than one little sister in oral salaciousness slinking around here somewhere.

This theme park must be one of those European outfits. In God-fearing countries, virgin maidens are not permitted to go around unbrassiered. And I'm feeling a bit leery of the tubular item she's pouting in her mouth.

Plus, regular New World boys don't sport bouffants. Someone beautified your follicles. Someone Euroed you. I can empathize with the look of mortal horror/sexual tension on your kisser.

Here "seduce" is used the double way that they in days gone by said "die."

54

These oft-thieved verbs, respectively transitive and in-, come fraught with
connotations, little or big. Take your pick. But don't keep it. You'll get caught.

For example—

    I, for one, was content to do
    my Niece/Step Daughter Boogaloo
    opposite your One Who
    Cries in the Intercranial Wilderness.

        How was a forest girl supposed to guess
        that, under desert Salome's headstrong salver,
        white phosphoric glands were testes-tucked
        which Uncle/Daddy milks like rattler fangs
        for enzyme slobber, to deflesh infants'
        outflanked floating ribs?

          As I played the wish bone contended for
          in that Holy Hungry Family tug-o'-war,
            I came to see that "come" and "kill" may
              struggle and writhe together in a single
          compound predicate. They could
tangle any minute, if one of the subjects
provisionally tagged "you" and "I" turns into, say,
for example, a black widow.

        That can't be ruled out. Every marital
          status is up for grabs here, as well as
            every superficial hue. Not to mention phylum.
Already a certain someone has grown an
arachnid's number of limbs, if not yet legs.

        Flippers would be no great shock.

      As for "Fin," the word will only arrive
          with one of our little deaths.

So I ask again—

Whose lower extremity's fixing to plunge
prosthetically down to de-cherry our prairie?

Make it another riddle:
Via what vesicle,
what ductis deferens,
might such vitality
duck down the pedal
pee-hole so pictured?

I invite you to unravel yourself.

Look up reluctantly once more
with less ambition than before,
but more subclavian
circumspection.

Note a three-cornered trope
such as crassness projects
on fatigued da Vinci daubs.

> Like a hop-jostled marsupial embryo slug,
> you may now migrate milkward
> from unpeekabooed nether pouch.
>
> Up louche loin, between meat pleats,
> steer clear, for pity's sake, of umbilicus,
> presuming its existence (parthenogenesis
> cannot be responsible for such a mess as this,
> and we fucked off from Eden two stations ago).
>
> Trace Momsy's hypotenuse up
> unfortunate thigh, regrettable gut.
> Triangulate on mammary papillae,
> the distended tips thereof.

In the inverted and reversible, not to say perverse, manner of procedure around here, teats suck instead of arsy-versy. Flow is reversed, going in the nipples, up into the net of veins and stretch marks. Local paps consume babies, like thunderbolts drawing subatoms from ambient element.

So, go ahead—

    Unsphincter that inner polymorphous pervert.
    Be up-vacuumed like lactose refluxed.
    Get aspirated as though post-nasally,
    through an accordioned breast pump

        Up you go,
          breakfast Milquetoast,
           breadbasketed Moses,
            undergo osmosis,
             into the tangled
              thrombotic gore-tubes,
              the striae distensae
               that grotesquify further
                this amputee's gravity-
                ravaged boobs.

        Let me rub your kisser in Chubby Mommy,
         all the way down to your earliest first-thingie-
          in-the-morning kitchen-sinky-winky
          bath time feet-balls:
         deep into past-epidermal-due-date
       overripe sour curd dispensers,
      skin-scum extensions--

--in and under, around and through and every
other preposition of place, to be discharged,
in electric ways, out the unnatural appendage
        in question, and back again, round and
          round.

With all this proximity,
      I knew we'd soon cycle in synchrony,
        you and me.

I reckon only one of us will come out, humanness intact.

                * * * *

You'll take comfort in being informed that we're not baby alligators.

    Neither of us sprang, a scale model,
    from jaws of a mini-replicated forbear.
    Somatology's not destiny around here.

That would be visually boring, in addition to implying cause and effect—a bad pun on our turf.

    Neotony's a sarcasm in our phylum.
    If horn worms retain false eye-glints
    when morphing to sphinx moths,
    likewise we must bear stigma,
    however modified in transit,
    that recap cumulative karmicities.
    It's just a matter of recognizing same.

Say, for example—

—one of us displays, like a garish mating crest, an attribute which, in general shape, resembles a steady flow of regurgitated blood, coagulated, mineralized like lava, molten gold brought up from the vulgar earthen duodenum—

—but the cone of metallic hemorrhage is inverted, its flow reversed, in accordance with regional statutes, so that the spreading-out is angled up insolently, in mockery of the flaccid funnel soon to flop down and damply fellate the Kansoid plain as through a rubber hookah tube—

—then the perplexity presents itself:

If someone empty-handed leads rats astray,
for this Piper, varicosally Pied, who plays?

Through what artifact, no pipe, but horn,
is the hextuple polyrhythm not sucked, but blown?

If shape can clue mouther's moniker,
can also the outward, as opposed to inward flow?

Which of us expels, which retains?

Who has previously vomited blood
and exhausted photons from the phiz?

Who has sucked smoke, ingested jizz?

Who's oral, and who's anal?

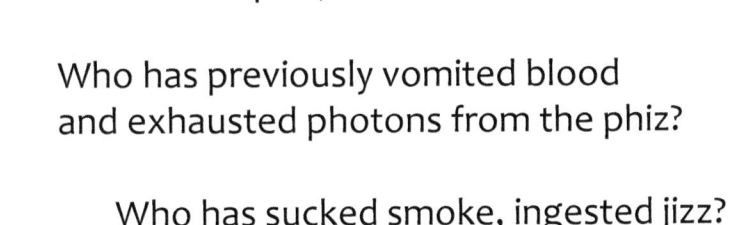

(The latter modifier is not to be construed on an exclusively literal basis; please recall that the Sacrosanct Source of Flux Eucharistic was earlier broached in the context of menstrual synchrony.)

>Whose scalp's been exposed
>more than half of the time,
>up till the quiddity called,
>facetiously, "now"?

I mean, not counting

Calliope's Boy—

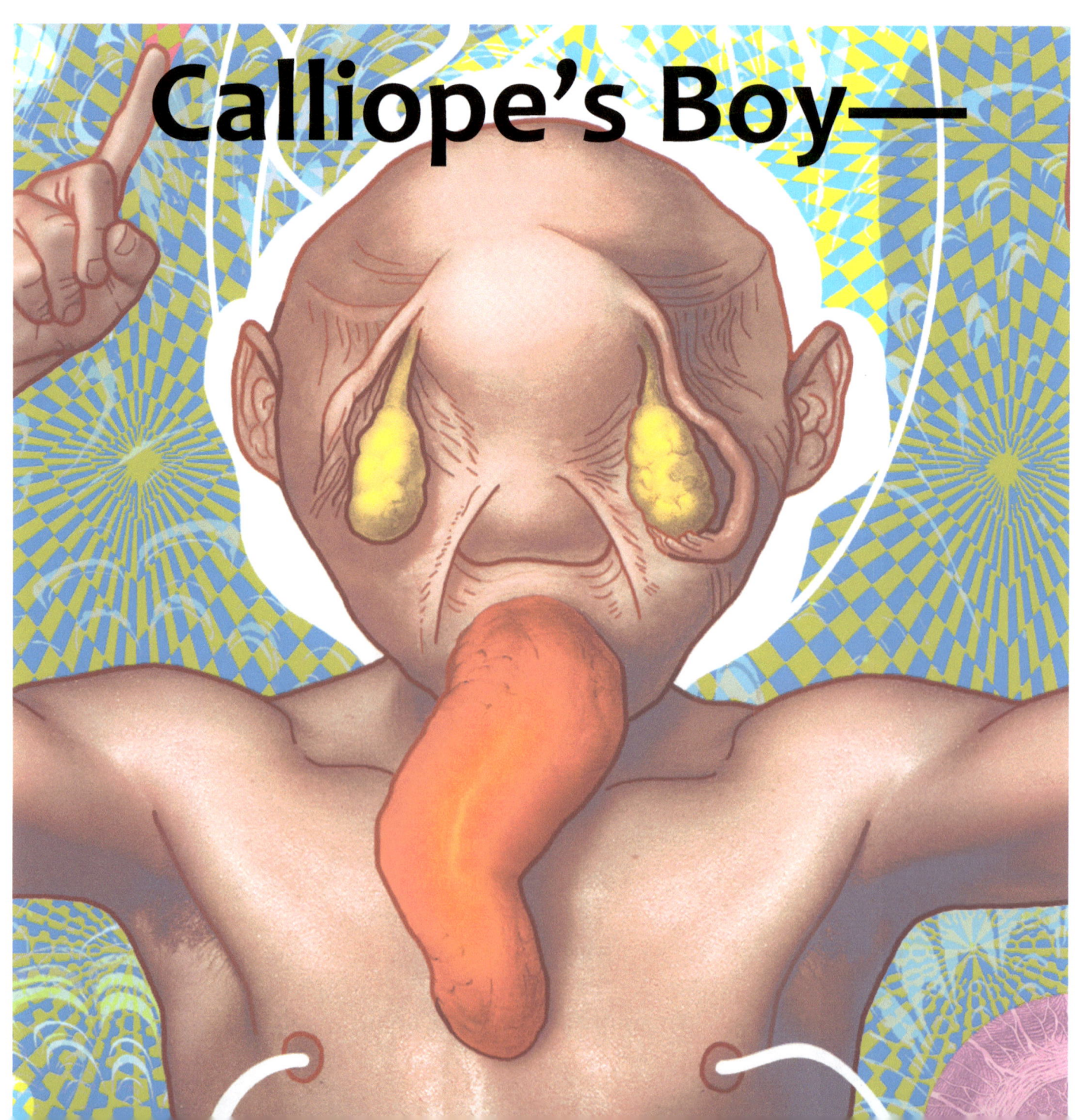

Who has logged job experience transmogging into an oversized god-apparent—I mean, during our previous dual-yoked simul-incarnation, during which—

> —who was appreciably bigger than whom?

As opposed to a certain other someone who, as far as can be ascertained, has only been an infant and a 'tween, though one at a time, and not in chronological order.

I could be a black widow next—might already have been ("sequence is not known in limbo," as the lady says); and I can take that in octuple stride. But I'd sooner be an unleggedly limp wormlet than spin among protean denizens who scorn—

> The One Basic Law Immutable

—and expect someone (emphasis on "one") like me to keep up.

> Call me an old-fashioned girl,
> call me not 'tween but 'tard,
> a reactionary stick in the manifest mud—

—but I still struggle with somatic plurality.

> Specific location, I've ever assumed,
> should remain the bare-naked minimum
> requirement for incarnation:
> the Anchoring Barrette in this mussed
> hairdo of a universe, legislating thus:
>
> No more, and no less,
> than one continuous carcass
> at a time per center of consciousness.

Tell me, if you can with a straight face (emphasis on the singular), there is no violator nearby of—

Commandment Eleven

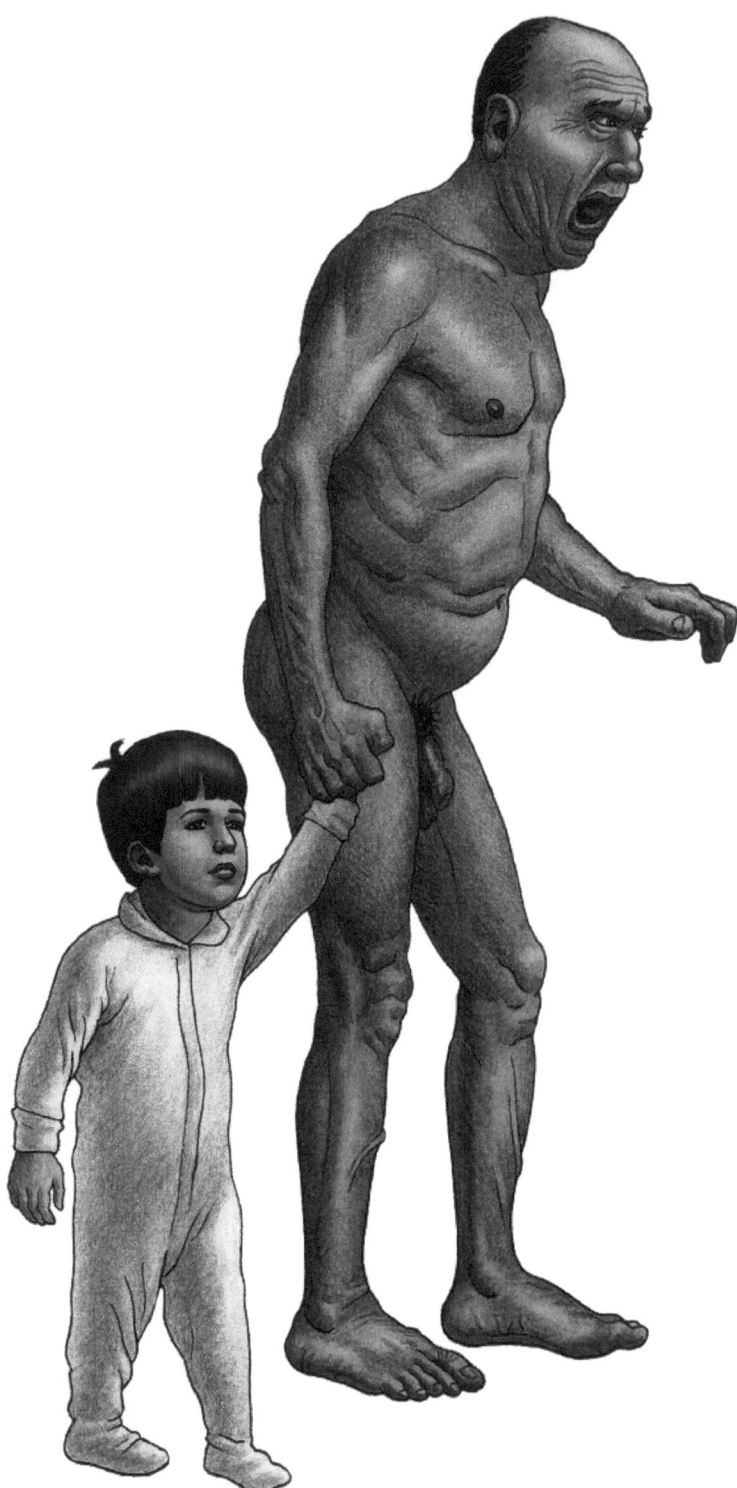

The all-engrossing Rigmarole
we use to rig our Weltanschauung,
our Liturgy Rigvedical, Decorous,
the Ground Rule coextensive
with the shifting self-dunes
that have ever constituted us,
all the long way from waterfall
to infernal magma barf-fall
to this Kansoid rainfall,
and back again, and forth—

—state without equivocation
(in rudimentary rhythm
that aids reception
of primeval wisdom)
as follows:

If the Hermetic Laws,
for example, be seven,
this is given:

What seems one, or four,
or three, or more
must be two.

Beyond both
a duel's a brawl.
"Come" and "kill"
descend to dull incontinence.

First person, second as well,
but no more, in essence.

Shaky senses of self, granted. But please note that, up till now, regardless of the quantity of extremities that have pranced before your eyes—

> —or trunks that have hulked,
> or necks that have gulped,
> or the lack thereof—

—only a single pair of more or less humanoid heads has occupied each frame (with, of course, the notable exceptions that prove the rule). And I think—okay, I hope—that each has been filled, if not necessarily to the brim and burgeoning out the ears, with a solitary psyche.

There. We've established the quantity if not quality of "who" as untentatively as anything can be established in these parts, which admittedly is not very.

Thereby is automatically mooted the last word of our catchy title: the "whom" with which you've been familiarized and mesmerized by its melodious recapitulation in the catch phrase that so effectively terminates each of our chapters. (Actually, I think they should be called Cantos.)

> The answer might be tooted
> in the organs that, till now, one of us lacked.
>
> What do you hear under the thunderclaps?

With remote charity and a ritual wink, it might almost be called mus—

Well, actually—

> —if you dare call it what I almost thought,
> do so in a whisper drowned beneath thunder.
>
> Follow the sibilance by numbered spits
> over the left shoulder, to propitiate Euterpe
> for such blasphemy.
>
> If "music" (in commas no less apotropaic
> than inverted) urges youngsters on
> in a cosmos unbemerded by rock
> (other than the living or liquid kinds),
> it must be a march.

Rhythmically this tune should walk.
But it waltzes, in arithmetic paradox
standard for these unaccountable parts.

There's a similarly perplexing reason why the arrangement is so tight. But, before I furnish you with that, I must say a word or two about this Third Station's—

Lady Paramount

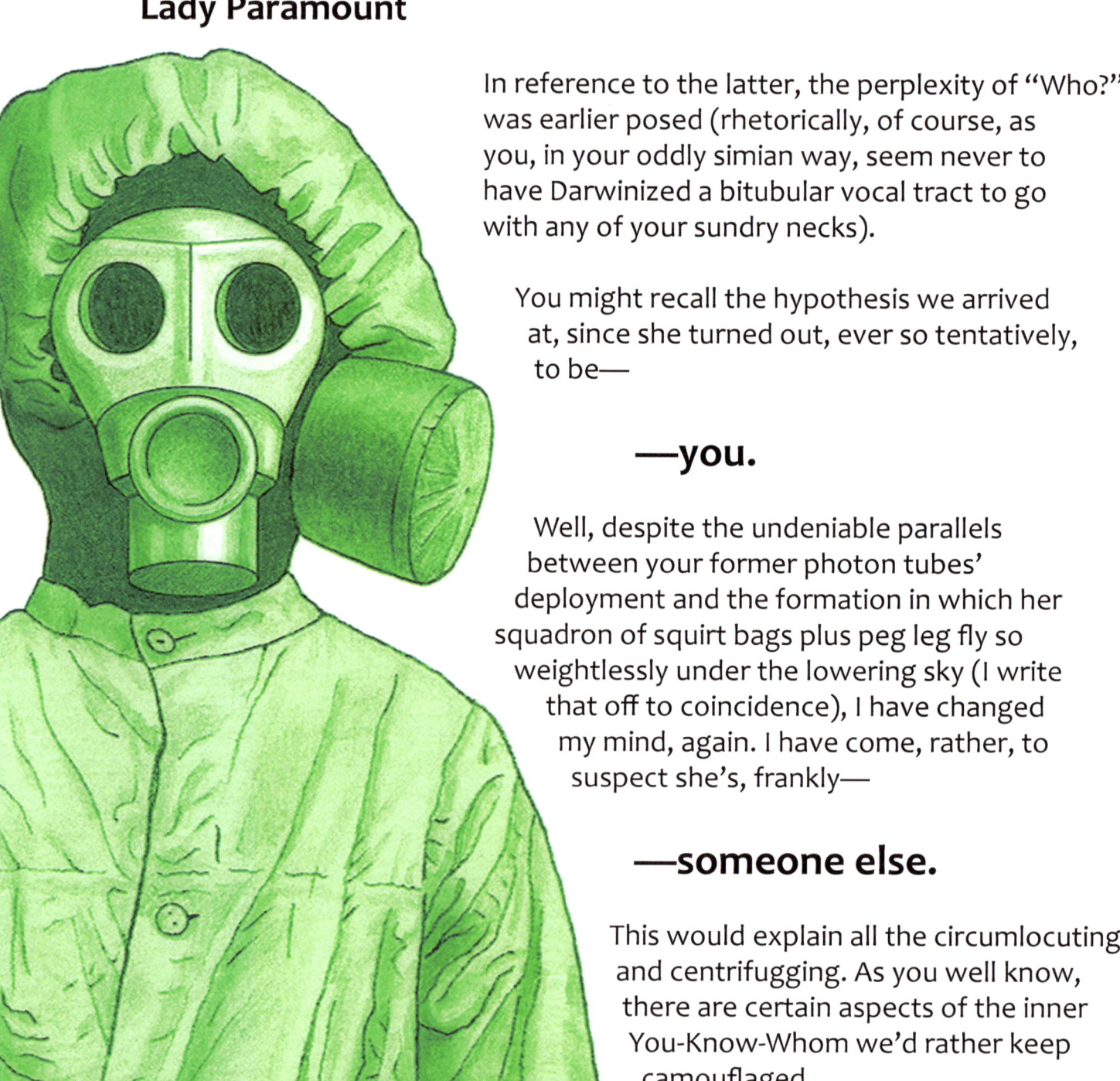

In reference to the latter, the perplexity of "Who?" was earlier posed (rhetorically, of course, as you, in your oddly simian way, seem never to have Darwinized a bitubular vocal tract to go with any of your sundry necks).

You might recall the hypothesis we arrived at, since she turned out, ever so tentatively, to be—

—you.

Well, despite the undeniable parallels between your former photon tubes' deployment and the formation in which her squadron of squirt bags plus peg leg fly so weightlessly under the lowering sky (I write that off to coincidence), I have changed my mind, again. I have come, rather, to suspect she's, frankly—

—someone else.

This would explain all the circumlocuting and centrifugging. As you well know, there are certain aspects of the inner You-Know-Whom we'd rather keep camouflaged.

I mean, she's someone else
other than any of youse.

Don't start with the nostril flares.
Spare me the voluptuous grunts.
Leave off the Fire Pillar glares.

You got to be Rhadamanthus,
immediately previous to this
(if tenseful time can be told in these parts).

So now it's someone else's turn to get big.
Someone else gets to be naked again,

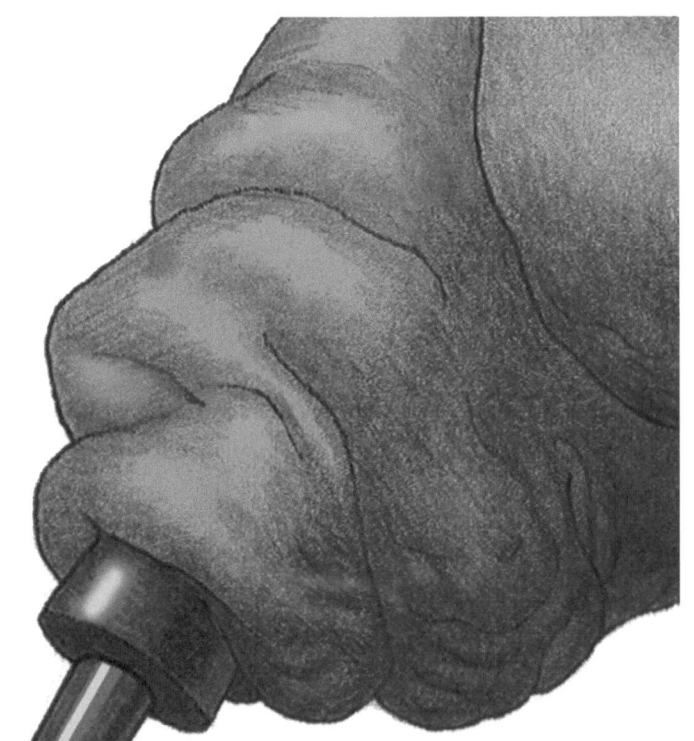

                        re-stripped bare as Moloch's
                        basted brat-morsel—
                        but now (indicating primacy)
                        unswaddled with gore.

And the presence of hairdo, good,
brunette, still topmost, unmussed,
steadfast–all the more precious for
having been shorn when your rival
played micro-Samson to your double
 Delilah—establishes the legitimacy
  this someone's claim to—

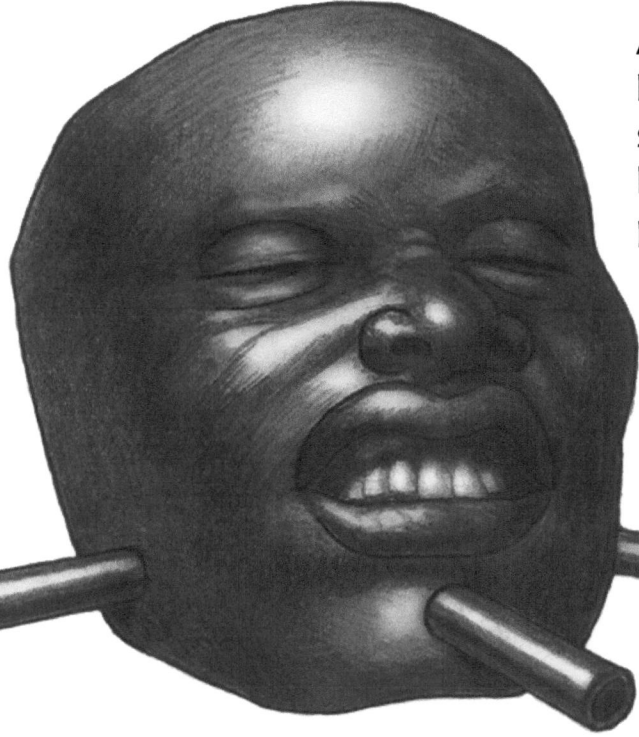

The Quality of Conductrix,
The Great Fecundating
         Go-Between of Heaven and Earth,
         the Mediatrix Electromagnetical,
       triple-time trailing clouds of—

Love Objective

—in this particular panel of our multi-tych.

Know what let's do?

Fun? Too bad. In fact, I insist.

    If this big mamacita be
    (yes, that's right) me,
    triply transfixed,
    maybe I'm subsuming you,
    presuming, daring to disequip you.

    Have I untied your tubes
    and whisked them away?

    Or would it be to delouse
    your phonetic parasites,
    so that in some subsequent station
    of our Passion Play
    you might separate your jaws
    (however many you've sprouted by then)
    and shift the point of view
    and speak for yourself?

Maybe then we'll find out the answer to this:

    Since she's me,
    who remains,
    in this frame,
    for you to be?

WE'LL SEE WHO SEDUCES WHOM.

CANTO VI.

**No more, and no less
than one continuous carcass
at a time per center of consciousness**

Time gone by—

    —a Jewish judge
    with a jawbone fetish
    got his muscled ass
    shaved and bound
    by the Proverbially Crass
    to their frangible version of—

The Pillar.

    My noggin, too, once was smooth
    and unhaired as his, a spermatozoon
    headed for a pellucid zone,
    babyish only outwardly,
    propelled by a teensy flagellum
    like a furtive hair grown back.

    Baby couldn't help but do
    a diploid of you—and then some.
    Baby cleaved the zygote temple
    down around your—rather, my—ears.

    I exploited a scalp discontinuity
    to expose skull tectonics
    and spread an upside birth canal
    for an entity (make that plural)
    to be thought through, like a virgin
    fontanelled from her unself-replicating
    Daddy/Twin's split brain-pan—

—in yet another of the alternative lifestyle choices comprising Family Life's burgeoning panoply, freely chosen in such all-inclusive liberal irrealities as ours.

Talk about a tough divorce! What a migraine. Mr. and Mrs. Yahweh-Asherah, you folks split up—

—twice. An illegal separation. What ever happened to—

> "No more, and no less,
> than one continuous carcass
> at a time per center of etcetera"?

Forget the letter of the law. You're in violation of the punctuation.

> Back in the postlapsarian broiler
> how was a mere neonate babbler,
> so primitive as to go undiapered,
> to predict that unisexed Auntie Papa,
> already half-assedly halved—
>
> —would halve yet again, into a passel
> of my parthenogenic cousin/siblings,
> whom I herd now, a corn-gorged gaggle
> of foix-geese and gras-ganders
> across the monocultured waste?

They (who?) say getting youngsters to march in a straight line is like herding certain even lower mammalian forms. But I would be surprised to see one of these musickers bolt far afield. To my eyes they're like several tennis balls strung in one nylon stocking, identity's flexible force field.

At first you were one, then two, pretty near. Now, third time out, you're four. Who had eight limbs, total, now spiders so many legs alone. I call that geometric, if not progression under the lowering sky.

> If such is the trebly nailed mockup
> on this sky-riven place of the skull,
> we might have six-plus-sixty
> percent of astonished Marys,
> but twice the Beloved Disciples.
>
> If the famous rice grain doubled
> on all sixty-plus-four squares,
> I'd better mate you pronto
> in this, our checkered career,
> before universal hunger ensues.

If at present I appear stout
and sufficiently overweening

to be the head-offing Queen,
it was yours, not mine,
as I recall, that rolled.

You'll be happy to know it's bounced back with a vengeance. You're—

—ambiguous Alice who leads with her phallus,
maraca-testicles shaking loose.

On the heels of her homologue scrotum,
symbolically-no-wider-than-long
(sole yonic requirement): the vulva drum.

Don't look askance at that last
component. Your four youngsters
sprang from Hermaphrodite,
hence the presence of anima
as well as her -mus.

And, bringing up your rear—

The single unifying factor
of all us sentient wretches
from annelid to costive Pope,
embodied existence's sole singularity
(apart from cake holes,
also standard issue).
Spastic-twitched, bangling,
those are cymbalettes
that were its hemorrhoids.

Meet the band: Prick Lad, Balls Lass, Cunt Boy, and,
backing them up on tambourine—Anus Girl.

We are, indeed, as He of Hippo said,
born between urine and excrement.

Especially you, over-qualified crotch on parade.
Thus is undermined a chthonian godlet's integrity.
You were the proudest angel, but now you're
scatterbrained centaur junk, to be tiptoed
around in the lower flats of our frame.

That must have hurt. You must be prostrate
on the inside.

Have I done the killing seduction yet?
At the very least I have face-raped you.

High time, I reckon, to vocalize over
fresh kill like a bitch lion, to raise
my mighty rightness and self-
hymn as, Lady Paramount, I sail!

Such numinousness I exert
on the initiate sensorium!
My chiaroscuro death-charges
by the back, from sacroiliac
via withers, up neck-nape
and out the jaw in trumpet jolts!

Such humbling sensations shine
in the unparaphrasable Upper Part of Mine,
which I can't yet self-impart,
not even with four unhuffed consonants.

Time to draw back the veil,
ride out on the rails:

The Physiognomy Ineffable!

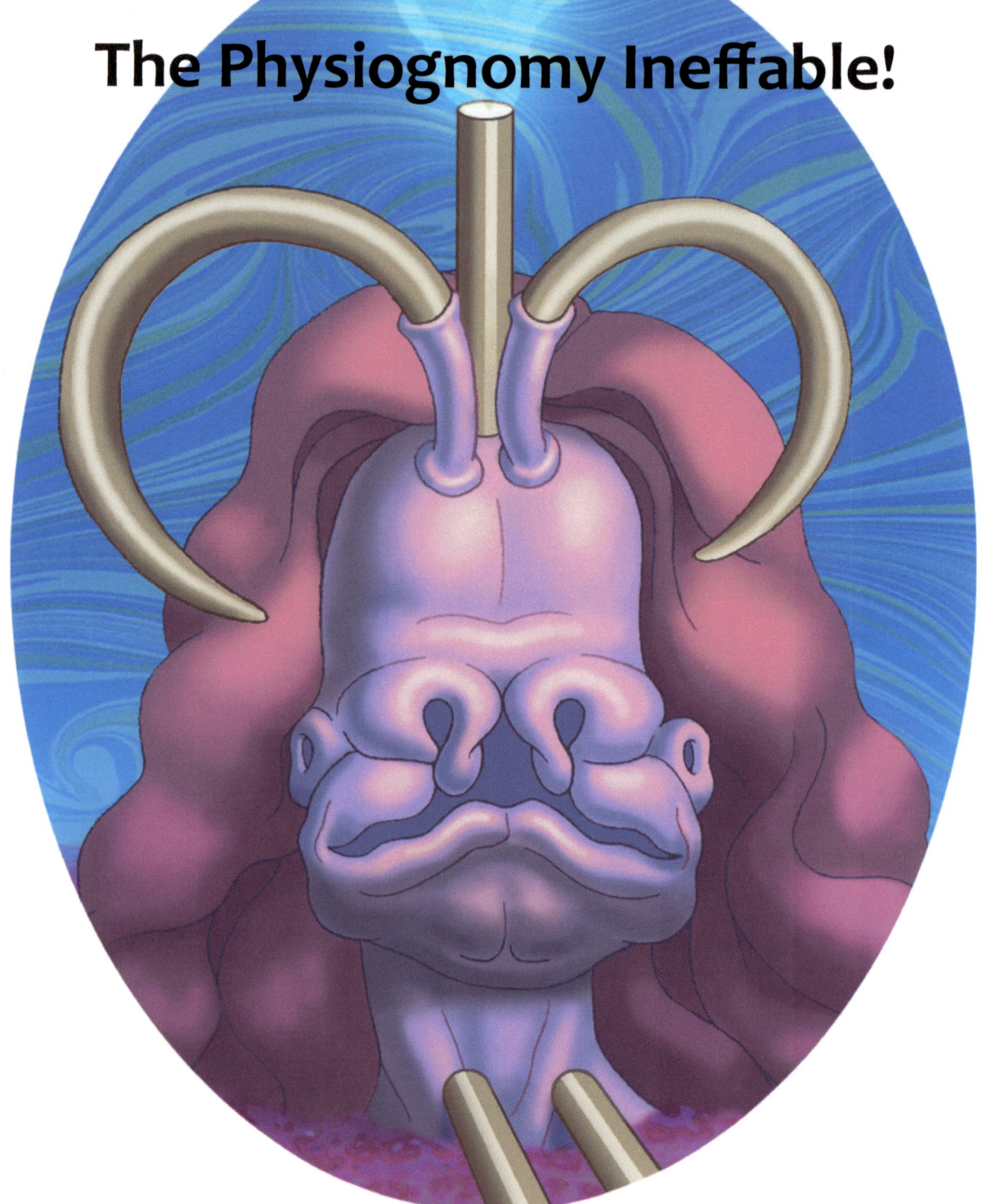

Shudder and secrete at Theophany!
Moon-sized, sun-eclipsing Me!
Floating unperturbed, I,
  above kiddy-skitter, nether-gallop
My Self through climate of high opinion!

Does the iris- and pupil-challenged condition of my eyes bode ill, or benignity, or disinterest?

Do I herd, or race, or pursue?
With my instrumentality raised high,
do I shield or goad or bless or crush your head?

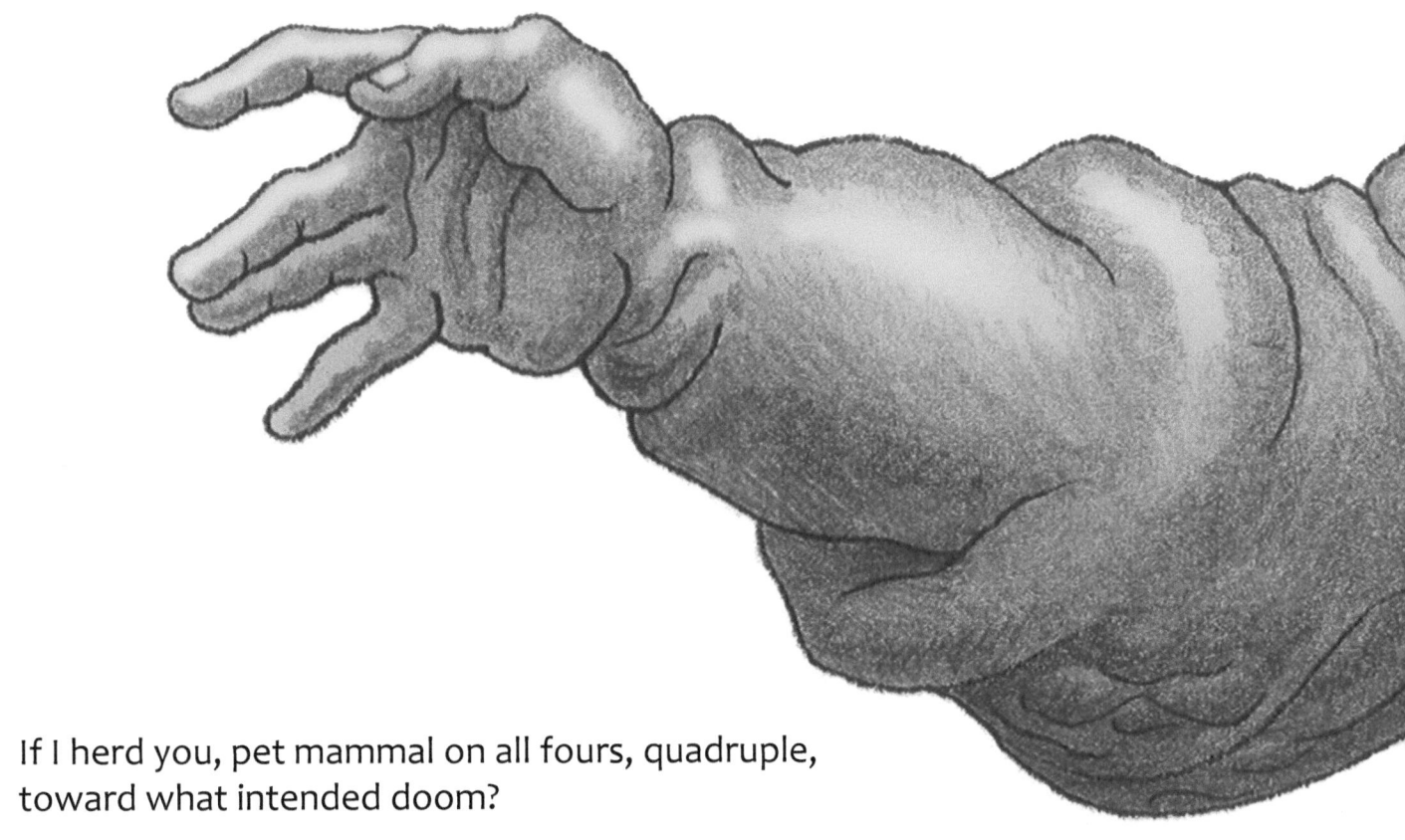

If I herd you, pet mammal on all fours, quadruple,
toward what intended doom?

WE'LL SEE WHO SEDUCES WHOM.

CANTO VII.

You never were entirely four-square behind the Phylum Chordata. Not in your selection of jointed appendages, at any rate.

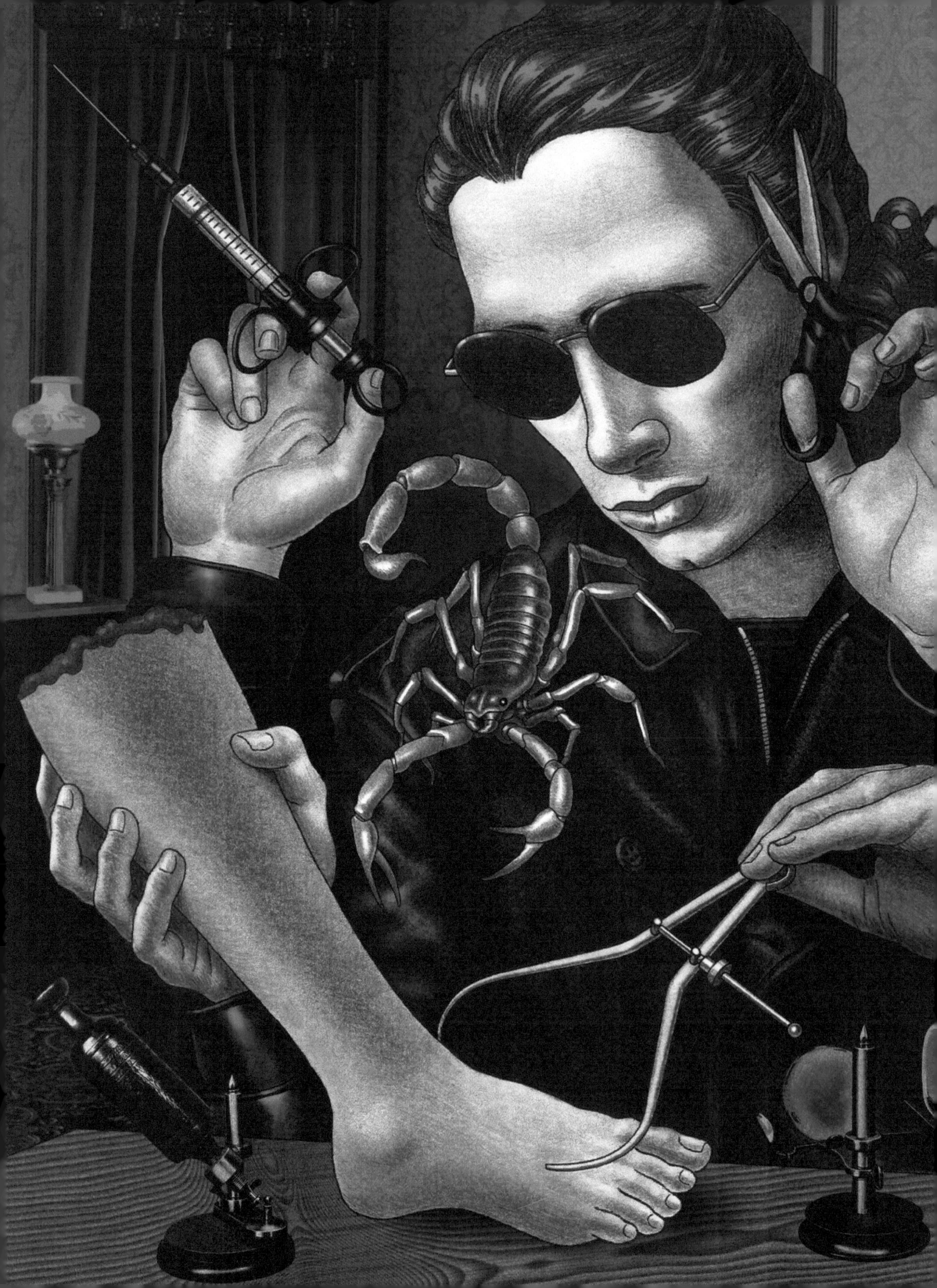

My pet mammals' heads are suddenly thumbs.
Fingers have sprung from their sixteen limbs.

    Each of their instruments is now another
    (except for the shank-and-trotter
    pincered front and center).

    The former tool of the late Prick Lad,
    once poked up and expulsive,
    has become the Dread Doodad
    that squirts and stabs.

Not much change in orientation, either: insolently angled as before.

    Any Lass put in charge of testicles
    soon grabs scissors, a pair.
    These clatter in the air
    like a similar quantity of maracas.

As is logical, we continue to catalog clockwise.

    Calipers bear down either side
    like a right and a left labium,
    or sticks that beleaguer a bass drum
    belly-borne by a gynologous Boy.

    If I say so myself (and I think I hear me),
    it blends without seam, this narrativity.
    It screams cohesion. But it's undestined
    to be shaped without one end rough-hewn.

    The remainder must be The Shadow
    or, by elimination's messy process,
    the Jungius Animanus–unless
    I mix my Metaphor Viennese
    with my Swiss cheesiness.

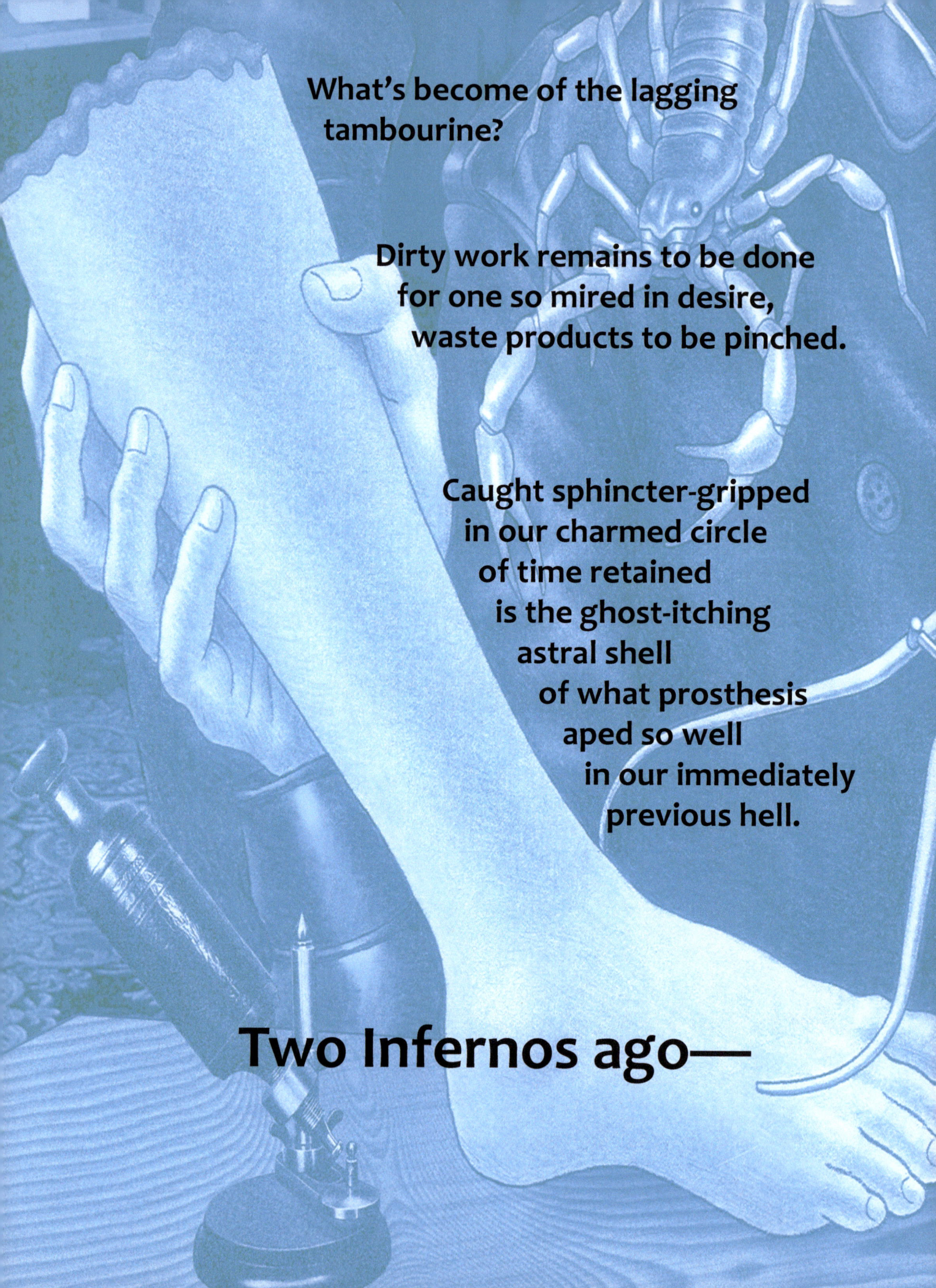

What's become of the lagging
tambourine?

Dirty work remains to be done
for one so mired in desire,
waste products to be pinched.

Caught sphincter-gripped
in our charmed circle
of time retained
is the ghost-itching
astral shell
of what prosthesis
aped so well
in our immediately
previous hell.

Two Infernos ago—

—as I lay, a gore-swaddled
species of babe in your sundry arms,
neonatally green in the fickle
head-fucks of the fontanelle,
I'd have scoffed soprano babble,
or at least burped red milk,
if someone (who?—there can be no other)
had sidled through underfoot lava
and insinuated to my infantine hear-hole
that, after a season of Kansoid normalcy—

—ex-Yahweh Unprepuced,
deposed Scrotal Sinai Boss,
would shake the hay dust
from whatever mutations hide
under this maple veneer,
and revert to his single-minded
yet duplicitously armed habits.

You never were entirely four-square behind the Phylum Chordata. Not in
your selection of jointed appendages, at any rate.

Little man, you must remain
so fixed on your raw brain
as to disdain all locomotion,
unless you plan to drop
your while-beguiling clatter-toys
and ply those pretty digits hoof-wise
to clop like a mammal in a surgical shop,

I must say it feels wholesome to return to the head count that proverbially improves upon singularity. And, though your armpits be ever so crowded, I am relieved to report the normal quantity of shoulders (as opposed to zero or four or eight).

    But look!

What do I see on your right one?

Something stunning in double entendre!
Something coiling with Love Objective!
Something gaudy and complex as sex,
or a sable garment's platinum dander!

    Partner! Death rassle-mate!
    Fellow wayfaring stranger-than-thou!
    Monozygotic butt-buddy of mine—

—you must have done something right in a previous panel (I don't think it involved melody, rhythm or harmony) to be ridden by so good an angel!

What altruism did you heist when I wasn't paying attention? How did you rack up sufficient gold stars to boast such a swoon-engendering lapel pin, such a gem-plated brooch? Little man—

    —under the waterfall, time gone by,
    as you tried not to roll off your rock,
    when you fed those poor jaw leeches,
    secreting them phonemic lactose–

    —the Karma Book Up Yonder
    surely tallied you merit on a par
    with those exhibitionistic acts
    of sub-Saharan starveling suckling
    which past-due-date cinema slatterns
    squirt from bags nobody would cringe
    to videotape in any other context
    (we've had our share of those lately)—

—for you now to rate such a familiar spirit,
perched so proudly, so prettily,
on your person.

And, how strangely familiar this spirit is.

Guess who.

Here's a hint in the form of self-quotation:

> "What seems one, or four,
> or three, or more
> must be two."

I'm flabbergasted no less than you!

> At your service.
> Your reified conscience, reporting for duty,
> your nostrum-stridulating Jiminy sidekick
> your nay-whisperer daemon.

And glad I am (yes, it's me), for a change—

> —to be a light burden shouldered
> rather than appetite-object fingered,
> wish-boned, basted, scarlet vomit-bastardized
> in subsoil picnic barbecue.

Glad, as well—

—to shed those fatigued, sebaceous leathers,
to cease spraining my stub among tillage.
Glad to be out of the pre-tornadic gloom
that blackens the drape-gap in back
and suffuses the inventory
of this John-Dee chamber, our first interior.
(Did someone say, "Get a room"?)

I invite you, through the corner of one sunglassed eye, to observe me as, with uttermost competence, in my shiny new person, I demonstrate—

    —genetics' handmaidenship to karma
    continuing my erstwhile sadhana:

    Still serving as gooseherd,
    straw-bossing lesser beings,
    I'm conducting, as always,
    your quartet in four movements,
    this time with von Karajan pedipalps.

    The caterpillar has huffed too deep,
    aspirated its cocoon and up-lungered
    not the expected color flutter,
    but an arachnid's prideful octo-swagger.

Not the projected black widow, true, but close enough to electrify the central nervous system with my own uncanny prescience in the previous chapt—I mean, Canto. Once more I must crave your indulgence as I—

Auto-Epiphanize!

Again, it's me-nee-Mamacita!
Even utterly motion-free,
poised to wiggle my ass
in my heart-stopping way,
still as illumination
in revealed scripture margins,
silently I throb and exude

the Polyrhythm Hextuple
your hick brats could only muddle
through the pesticide stubble.

I'm virtuoso Kundalini
personified, insectified.

I am the Spiral Force
with inbuilt stinger,
shoulder-deployed
to seduce the inner Roosky
out of your noo-sky.

Constellation Heaven-Born,
loved by the same sidereality
that numenized, humanized Mamacita,
limbs burnished as an igneous bauble,
I yearn to fornicate with my sublime self,
to auto-neurotoxicate.

Who needs a prettifying barrette when, topmost, you've got a ponytail, unmussable, exoskeletal? With Nether Parts hypertrophied and ultra-peekabooable as mine, I know you're looking where you shouldn't—why else the shades? How else to explain the envenomed pussy-whipsnap pose I strike?

Does it tally as bestiality if it's with a bug?

Have we seen someone seduced? So soon?

    Was Xanthippe's live-in lout
    daemoned around by his Silenus snout,
    or arsy-versy? Jury's still out.

So beautiful am I—

    —burnished as an onyx hookah,
    poised, flexed to take tickling liberties
    with your atavism of androgyne cheek—

—that another element in the frame might easily go unnoticed behind my glamour glow (and I don't mean the period lamp on the sideboard).

With gracious bounty, permit me to draw attention briefly away from my sacralizing lineaments, and toward—

    The Presentation Self (yours).

I'd love to huff sweet phonemes in your ear—but how can I put this? I don't want to be rude.

Punctilious as you've been in your attempt at "impression management" (committers of social science have termed it so), you missed some details. Two, to be exact.

Little man, while shifting your sleek black skin from phiz to trunk, you seem to have dropped the inlets for speech so briefly won in plain state octuplicate. I must ask again:

Can you hear me?

Maybe earlessness is all the rage.
Skull-handles, turbulence inducers,
like warts of bird sauce on aerofoils,
do tend to spoil the flow of a 'do.

Who's brunette-coiffed now,
post-Hiroshima teen dream-style,
barretted no doubt, with waves so thick
they could conceal a cranium split for two?
No scalp discontinuity exposes skull tectonics.

If I correctly interpret the manner in which your carpet and wallpaper writhe with their own paisley animation, this is an Usher Chamber. The kit indicates a Victorianesque left-path lab.

Do I raise my tail upon Practical Occultism's Face of Choice?

The adolescence is no surprise
in this jail-bait worshiping age.
Mired in matter, desire,
impression is managed to inspire
maximum Eros in the commonest
low-down degenerator

Clear down to exquisite Cupid's-bow
your androgyne history purses and pouts,
unsmiling as one who lately giggled,
and twiddled toy tambourines,
is trying to live jangles and jigs down,
but has yet experienced nothing to frown about.

Chin no hairier than my ass
on blood baptism day,
erotically cleft, solitary pock
left by speech-leech
(Clearasil foundation, I'd say),
cosmeticized no less punctiliously
than your necrophilic podo-fetish—
also young, odorless, depilated, unisex.

    Polarized specs
    contain callowness
    more than screen sun
    of which there is none,
    hence goth pallor
    in this parlour
    out of Poe—

—himself no monument to the mind's maturation.

And, on those magickers, your pretty boy-girl fingers, not so much as a hangnail to witness pain, let alone the distension and amputation I bore as your kindergarten music teacher one panel, or so, ago.

    No naked godlings nor babies
    nor overgrown gnomesses here,
    just zippers and leather.

    This is regression,
    like all left-hand births,
    a fall deeper into matter.

    The disintegrating godlet,
    self-exiled among kit-clatter
    and clangor of kaboodle,
    can't tear himself from things of the skin,
    nor the torn-away flesh from his lower-right fist.

    Far above, on a more dextrous brink,
    someone ingenuous (a bug, I think)
    uttered aloud The Question Direct:

    "You? Who are you?"

    Maybe I've narrowed it down to two.
    Would Poet and Painter do?

Or maybe just a couple death-wrestlers, pro.

I could swear it's as though
Painter and Poet in tempera tights
and lexical testicle cup death-grapple here.

Try to pin me with (as opposed to upon) your shoulder.

I can break whatever hold you throw,
except, maybe, vulgarity.
Store-bought blood needs more ink
to wash than pigment to smear.

Kaboodle clangor,
jingle of pelf,
not self-delved
but fetched off the shelf.

Itemized price units, vendibles taxed,
in strict accordance with factory specs.
Such bric, such brac guaranteedly tacks
shopkeeperly spirits to existence.

Pockets are needed
for things to be toted
that don't come attached,
like unfalse teeth
or screwed-in prostheses.

Thumbs need opposing
to flexures of finger
so inventory won't drop
and shatter, cost-ineffective,
under your salesmanly nose
on formica veneer,
photographic maple grain,
the Universal Price Code
scanned by doodads
courtesy of Bunsen et fils,
on the table that obscures
the basement dirt—

—where you should be squatting and projecting instead, digging empty cup-handed for a shape purer than these.

A hint, a reminder of what we've been seeking all along:

> It's a bong. It's a shlong.
> It's a stub-compensator,
> a thunder conductor,
> a shared hypodermical
> vector of transpecies syndromes.

It makes tracks—but not the type sunk in puerility's black-leathered elbow, not those perivascular hematomas which recall, to the suggestible mind, the networks of puckers thrown in a visual net around the textures of certain outsized creatures' curd-bags.

> Unblunted by jabs in earth-crust,
> in gluten-field, in unbodied Ethiope chinbone
> where it leaks lingo, this suggestive shape
> fumigates cake-holes of thrill-seeking jail-bait,
> getting fetal dreams in cranial uteri,
> entheogenically.

> It materializes gagged double
> down Moloch's four collarbones,
> though oneirosis in such situations
> torques into throats
> this serviceable getter of bearings:

The Conduit Geometrical.

* * * *

Screwed through kinked bottlenecks
of Subcorticollective Uncorked,
till organic forms flutter
like Charmin on shoe heels—

—we'll soon have reached the last page of the Family Romance, clipped and
redeemed the karmic coupons among the back page ads, and tossed that cellulose-
based retail product aside.

With decreasing resolution, recurring by rote
in each of our routine dreams, the roll shall dutifully
be called per Canto:

Textbook Shadow, Presentable Self.
Next comes Animus and the -ma thereof
(as though, around here, they'd be distinguishable).

Halfheartedly out-Heroding Herod
in the Daughter/Niece department,
Auntie Momsy, Creon's sis,
will repeat her journeymanlike cameo
with her nearest propinquity,
or maybe come lactatingly on
like Vag-Dent.

Double check. Are we de-neuroticized yet?

We must be. Look around the edges.
The frame's working through the furniture.

Soon enough—

—we'll have gone beyond 'tweens
and their semi-skilled blow jobs,
and the very biology that drives them
so damply, into headfuls of amphiboly.

Girly-poos no less
than Rhadamanthus
come with the dust,
and they're gone with the Manvantara
(overdue in any case).

Drilled under geology, we'll be deeper
than stone, including the uncongealed
retch of eight-foot Siamese chthonians
on their hemorrhaging way to extinction
in favor of pillars outright, maybe of
salt—something unliving at any rate,
yet crystalline, as peekabooed by a
plighted wife in hindsight.

Soon we'll be deep enough to hear
the music of the simple plasma spheres.

    Take a splash of hydrogen,
    add a quack of helium,
    plus a touch of self-gratifica–
    I mean, gravitation—

—then fuck off way past that, and that'll be me.

Also, presumably, you (though, you're not saying much,
so how do I know?).

Farted from the fundament
of Existence Herself,

    we shall plop in the Ideal Privy
    to spiral clockwise, also counter-,
    alongside the Immutable,
    the Orthogonal, the Parallelopiped
    and shit like that.

  Hexahedronic harpooners, us,
  harassing Mobius Turd,
  persistent objects
  minus the nerds.

The Tube, the Cuboid, surds
resolved, unleft in cube roots,
a lattice of atoms' vibrational props
only rotors, curves and simultaneity—

–was that a hashish hookah I
blew, or a clangy nitrous tank?

    Our location is likewise liquid,
    presence itself more unfixed
    than wormlets transfixed,
    unstiffed by spatial coordinates,
    themselves comprising
    the cylinder, the cuboid,
    superficially smooth,
    to shine with abstractions's
    highlights, self-similarly regular.

We'll have arrived at shapes that only
pre-exist, and will have shifted—

    —upgraded un-selves to the Form Realm
    of geometric if not precisely Platonic solids:

The Item Orthogonal
of hexahedronical onyx,
the burnished black parallelopiped,
earlier displayed, lately mislaid,
first and last espied topside
in a previous episode—
—the flaw in a mirror
that glimpses silver.

The cylinder, right-circular, not even elliptic
(as so much around here), solid as a cigarette holder,
paradoxically fastened to neolithic shapelessness,
poking schematically skeletal through fleshliness,
dissolving edges, the notion beneath the skin,
planted in the epidermal Prairie Ephemeral,
is as good an anchor as we'll need,
as solid a context—

—as, in succeeding panels—

Painter and Poet continue to rassle,
bodhisattvic, among representational baubles—
as I presume we'll do, since you're no Mondrian,
thank Brahma.

Pollock had the right idea—
if he'd only used a ruler.

WE'LL SEE WHO SEDUCES WHOM.

CANTO VIII.

**In order to make the time we spend sleeping more profitable, we must first recognize that we are dreaming
—Padma Shugchang**

When secret psychodramas of the night
initiate us in their mysteries,
a blindfold's tourniquetted and cinched tight
to swaddle up our eyes like infant twins
until they're ready to contain a glimpse
of chaos that surpasses all restraint.

The Lucid Dream will prematurely tease
that diaper from your exoteric face.

Tibetans taught this to their fledgling dead
before enduring death-by-Mao instead.
But dream yogins are just as doctrinaire
as Ratzinger in his sedilla chair.
And lately, when those Buddhist bardos gleam,
they're reinterpreted as something screened.

Halfwitted dreams with one shut eye are dreamt,
half-assed hallucinations semi-slept.
When waking thoughts are not exactly bright.
What makes us think they might illumine sleep?

Beneath those liquid crystal molecules
a glimpse of liquidated personhood's
horrific light is yet available.
Pure nothingness still seethes behind those screens
in pre- and post-existent harmony.
Dominions, Powers and Principalities
will show us their annihilating truths
unless they're mashed with asininity.

The Lucid Dream is self-endorsing, trite.
Do we presume to claim ourselves the right
to spread our own ephemerality
like acne sebum, oiling troubled waves
that otherwise dredge monsters up from depths?

The perishable citizen, the dreck
that's taken out and dumped when trashed by death,
assuming the high autocratic post
of Overseer General for Dreams,
exerts fastidiousness upon the Realm
where rot's unripe, bizarrerie the norm.

The consciousness, the primate's attitude,
entangled in its raveling rag of skin,
a function of the gonads' shamelessness,
projects its flesh dependency on thoughts
that under sleep parthenogenerate.

The personality, quotidian,
assumes it owes selfhood to parentage
and, therefore, on the masses of the night
obtrudes overt erotic imagery,
which super-egoistic scruples strip
of pricks and cunts and inhumanity.

To pass unindividuated time
connective tissue's caused to interlink.
Together two mere wads of stuff butt heads
and glue collaborative tongues to mutual tits
in furtive concert, toward no nobler end
than to bedungeon in organic cells
the sundry sprites who grace the ambient air.

It's doubtful that an exiled godly being
on temporary basis matter-mired
would call for fucking as prerequisite
instead of something far more pertinent
to spirits' unadulterated state:
hermetic isolation, strange, sublime.

Halfhearted plays for eyes with half-shut lids
are mounted without benefit of Id.
We're fornicating to a metronome,
restricting holocausts to hookah tubes,
hysteria to sighs of lassitude.
While gutting babies with a laser tool,
we cauterize and disinfect the wounds
before we've even had the time to drool.
Why would we want to will away the chance?

Because his dreams are emceed by himself,
the Lucid Dreamer looks upon the world
to presuppose a slightly larger Self
pulled from his ass: the most perfunctory
and shallow of all semi-gelled conceits.
The Popish Heavenly Father-cum-Prot God
is kidnaped from his Jewish tribal tent
and styled the Ultimate Reality,
himself the most egregious specimen
of Lucid Dreamer semi-dreamt by men.

Just as the Lucid Dreamer here below
puts on a prissy chicken liver show,
a celibate yet generative Lord
oviparized a teen's cloacal quim
in soft-boiled porno-mythopoesy
to violate his own presumptive laws
as priests transgress their juicy altar boys.

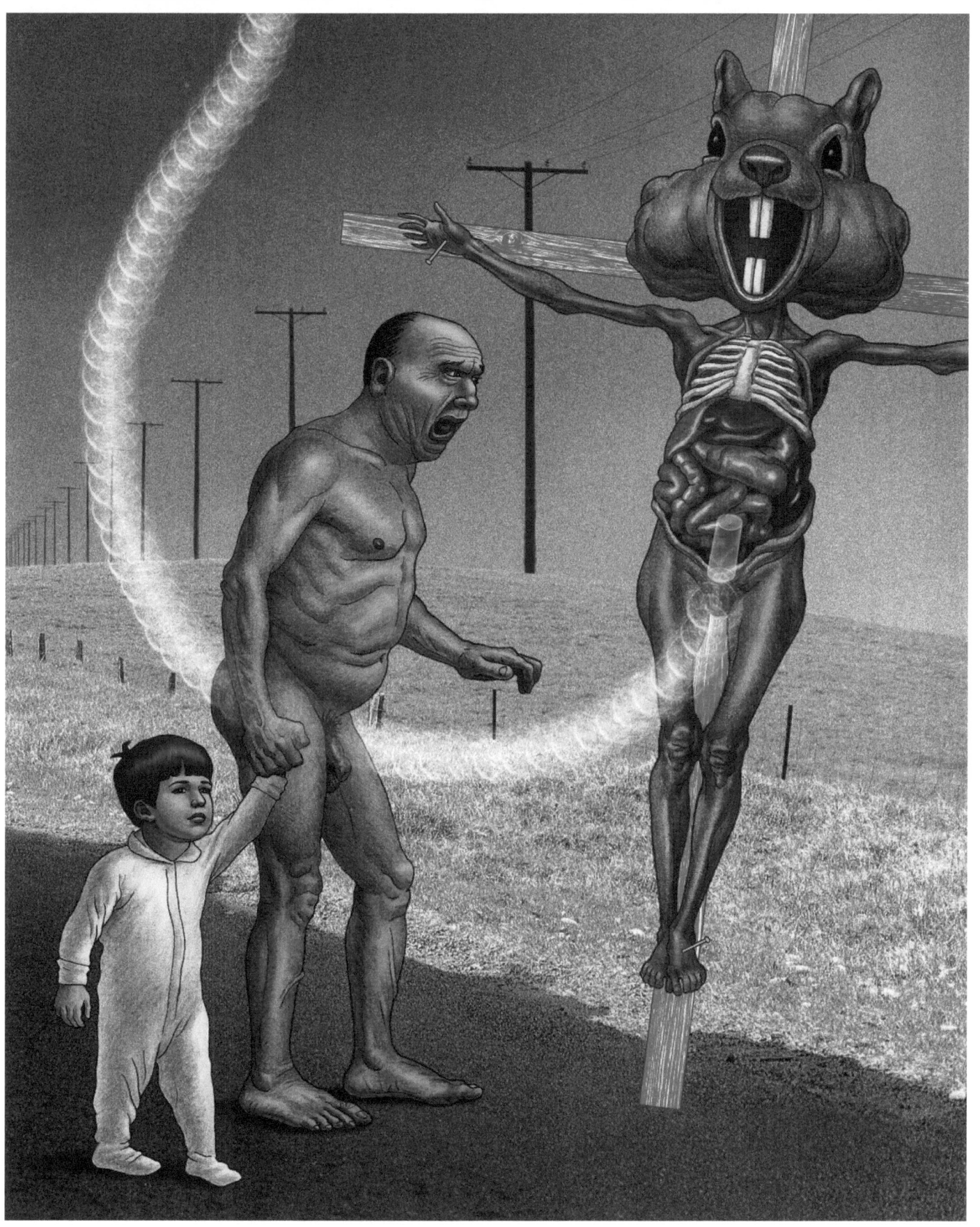

**Suffer the little children in their footie-jammies
to come unto the Easter Squirrel.
Take, eat, these are his sweetbread-kebabs.
"This is what will happen to you if you tell a soul,"
snarls Father Xavier.**

This Demiurgic errand boy, this mope,
gets gussied up as pretty as a pope.
To take this bungling spastic fucker-up
of our particular niggling solar clump,
and puff him into That Unthinkable,
unreachable by either praise or blame
entails the sickest blasphemy of all.[1]

The Ultimate Reality would scorn
to implicate its sacrosanctity
in perpetration of the cosmic botch
we childishly refer to as "our world."
It's sacrilege, in exclusivity
performable by Lucid Dreaming twats,
the crassest, the most ultra-obvious
of all counterintuitivities.

The stunted sense of immaterial things
that hampers him who never deeply sleeps,
whose Lorelei distracts him from dream work,
retards his rationality as well.
So, ears unstopped, he entertains beliefs
epitomizing all vulgarities.

To dream lucidity is to commit,
in argument as dumb as circular,
theodicies of cosmic tastelessness.
Vicarious atonement is contrived
when foolishness summarily denies
rebirth and karma's double principle
that manifestly runs the universe.
Eternal bliss or torment just as long
supplant probation, which justice demands.
That's Lucid Dreaming's tenseful time-yoked error.

Such asininity necessitates
a spiritual and moral travesty:
the filthy motto puked in Pseudo-Paul's
Epistle to the Hebrews (clearly forged):
"Die only once, and afterwards be judged."
For this we have the Lucid Dream to curse.

---

1 See Appendix.

As if it's not uncouth enough to try
to make Jehovah chief executive,
the Lucid Dreamer essays to dumb down
our Gnomes, our Undines, Salamanders, Sylphs,
our Elementals and their mighty ilk.
The cherub's terror is masked in baby pudge,
the Syrian Monstress forcibly shanghaied
to grace this world of Disneyfied pastel
with attributes originally belched from Hell.

Where fins and scales of wadded mud prevailed,
once wedged all round with hexed cuneiform
that hissed profundities as old as towns,
we get a glabrous tweeny's turquoise gown.

Would Atargatis pose for lucid eyes,
or would a single brief self-conscious glance
cause more than cock to swell and barf its brains?
Did she employ that fish tail as a tease,
a tickling adjunct to cartoonish tits,
or as cetacean scourge to smash to bits
the shivered shrimp boats of the human wits?

Her followers castrate themselves with shards.
Semiramis, her daughter, dorked a horse.
Somehow I doubt she'd be a slickened thing,
in face as featureless as mindless gets,
not even ill-considered, complacent,
pubeless as an Arab's promised Houri,
not bald, but depilated, with a scalp
equipped with polyvinylchloride coif
and nipples alien to dairy toil.
Gravity's repealed within their ken.

Ostensible pudenda, barbie-dolled,
are glossed beneath agenitalic thighs
perpetually pinched in pudency,
tempered to a Virgin Mary blue,
the surface texture purged of macula.

I perceived a mermaid in mid-splash among the waters... quite muddy, very disgusting... a bubbling mire... I was embarrassed for her... I pretended not to see her... I began to move away.
—Louis-Ferdinand Celine, *School of Cadavers* (anonymous translator)

A non-mammalian lower torso bleeds
when stroked by fillet knife, but not monthly.
Nigredo's black unshaped lubricity
gets socialized, elucidated, bleached
by exegesis, epidermis-deep.
Erased is vene varicose's bruise,
unpuckered the striae distensae.

I want my Megalo-Mestiza Ma,
although she was more difficult to draw.

The skivvied geezer flits like Peter Pan
and grimaces with appetite for tongue.
I'm not sure if he constitutes a Self,
or whether he's conjoined, coterminous,
    with this flip witch
    who would transfix
her sibling with a digit to the chin.
I do like that one extra mutant fin.
Its growth is strictly owing to my sin.

Time for heptametric mea culpas:

    I'm sorry to have emphasized
        the 'tween's orality,
    and that I conjured on your head
        the name of Asherah.
    Apologies are due, as well,
        for making such a stink
    of Mamacita's handicap
        and causing it to stand
    for things hyper-Platonical.
        Nor should I have begun
    that weird nonsense of counting limbs
        and making the norm eight.
    It doesn't mean I wanted you
        to recapitulate.

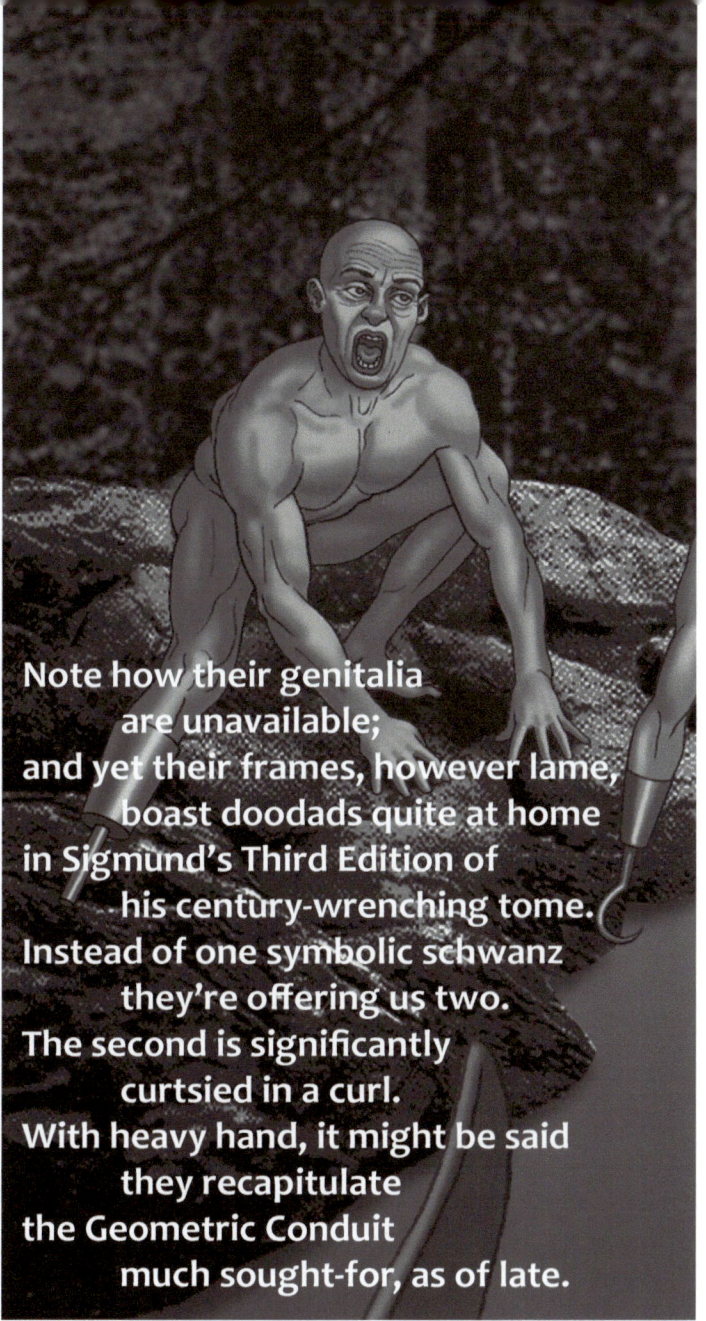

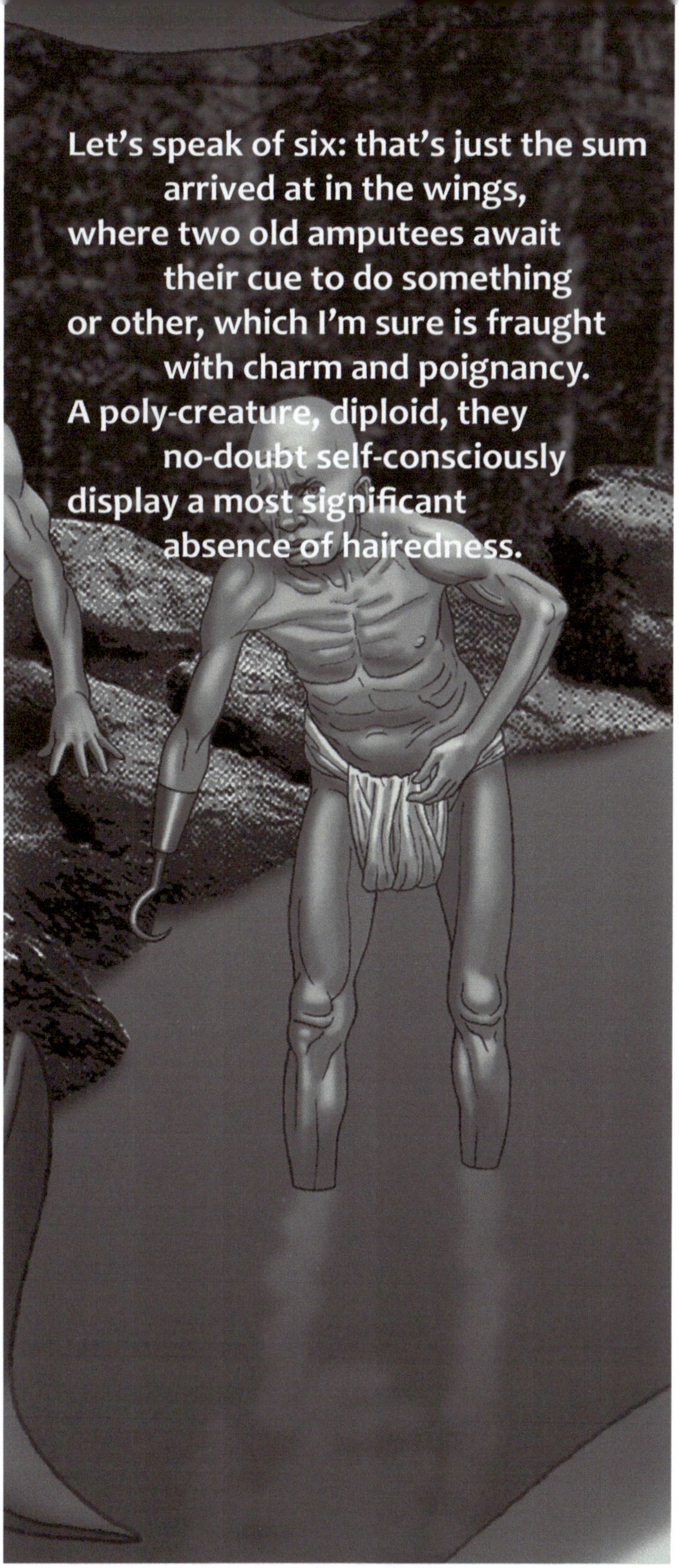

Note how their genitalia
    are unavailable;
and yet their frames, however lame,
    boast doodads quite at home
in Sigmund's Third Edition of
    his century-wrenching tome.
Instead of one symbolic schwanz
    they're offering us two.
The second is significantly
    curtsied in a curl.
With heavy hand, it might be said
    they recapitulate
the Geometric Conduit
    much sought-for, as of late.

Let's speak of six: that's just the sum
    arrived at in the wings,
where two old amputees await
    their cue to do something
or other, which I'm sure is fraught
    with charm and poignancy.
A poly-creature, diploid, they
    no-doubt self-consciously
display a most significant
    absence of hairedness.

Such bearings-getters would have served
    in Cantos before this,
when we were deep enough in sleep
    to whiff the rank abyss.
But now we're three-fourths wide awake
    to hackneyed workaday,
and soon ourselves will amputate
    our prostheses away.

Like all artists you've chained yourself
    to that Caucasian crag,
spread-eagled wide to feed the Muse
    affecting vulture drag.
She's fixed to ply her painted claws
    and steal the strangest gland
your painterly thorax can yield
    to colorize her nest.
But now and then that hideous hen's
    beaked inspiration flies
to vomit your cirrhosis down
    the throats of her fledglings.
Then comes the dreaming stupor when
    your palette gets redaubed.

Please don't reach out and switch me
    like your bedside radio.
Don't suffer me to bloviate
    and Limbaugh in your ear
with my syntactic sarcasm
    and lexiconic lies.
My idiosyncratic brand
    of Dream Lucidity
is only fit to cheapen Bradley's
    narrativity.

Unqualified to tell you what to see,
I fear your Lucid Dreamer has been me.
You're better off attempting to impose
strict pentametric iambs on the prose
that grunts from chimpanzaic nostril holes.

With both ears fastened tightly as your eyes,
just ignore my jokey doggerel snores.
The unexamined Dream Life's not worth waking.
You need your beauty sleep, your ugly more.

Dig underneath your frontal lobes
    to your reptilian core.
Find something inexpressible
    by word and metaphor,
in whose appalling shadow syntax
    grovels like a whore.

Please Yahweh-Asherah me
    on Mamacita's gallows.
You made it look so easy when
    you charged my pen with gall.
Give me something so immense
    It murders Lucid Dreaming.

White phosphorize my orbits both
    and damn me straight to Gaza.
Slam me in the dark like eyeless
    Samson on his pillar,
chained by Philistines and mocked
    by theriomorphic gods.
I tend to write my best when facing
    worse than even odds.

And if we choose to self-apply
    the Tantric metaphor,
persuade my Shakti shamelessly
    to shimmy on your schwanz.
We'll do the missionary style
    of all left-path adepts,
you motionless as stoned Lingam.
    I'll do the spastic nautch.

You needn't be "responsive to
    my needs" like some poor dork
who makes love like another chick
    instead of slamming pork.
When poking round for images
    that yield the joke, the curse,
it's not familiarity
    in which I must immerse.

> But still the question will remain
> 	of "Who seduces whom?"
> as we contest to see who'll be
> 	the first to overcome,
> or, in vernacular, will come
> 	till limp and out of breath.
> It won't be shown till one of us
> 	achieves the little death.
> This wrestling match won't hear full count
> 	till you, or I, astonished,
> vanquished by his brother's skill,
> 	capitulates—unless
> you "bring it with you when you come"
> 	as in the tavern song.

Then double murder-suicide combines
with synchro-spooge regurgitating wongs,
and, fighting, fornicating, consummates
this odd behavior we're dead-set upon.

> Until that time, from out of frame,
> like distant fireworks on display
> 	behind a screen of trees
> 	beyond will's ken, come hints:
> a strange arrival we must not
> prosodify, much less elucidate.

> Layered on a spectrum
> 	immune to our control,
> unmashed with asininity,
> blend and gleam such tints as fix
> 	what we once oxydized
> with officious ultraviolet squints.

Such impersonhood, liquescent, glimpsed,
	such unscreened seething nothingness,
	adumbrated unconsciously
		above, in Stanza Five,
	might seem, to exoteric eyes,
pathetically, fallaciously alive.

But it won't be tarted up,
this green obliquity, whose glow
 is hardly thinkable:
the ever-present hidden hint of That.

In unannihilating light,
polyvinylchloride shells assume
 an elemental numen,
expressed within the universe of green,
the ecosystem quickening the rock,
 astonishing, that seats your pretty
 mermaid's uncracked butt

 Mossy lichen's glow
redeems this whole pugnacious Canto.
 If not Geometric,
 it's Geological,
this bearing-ungetting iridescence
for which I, humbled, praise and thank
 your illucidity.

 You rightly have rolled over
and your REM has been resumed.

NOW WE WILL SEE WHO SEDUCES WHOM.

APPENDIX

...it became a thing such as even Dante could not have conceived...
—Mary Wollstonecraft Shelley

The emblematic monster of the age, our default thing that goes bump in the night, was given an airing, with full iconic attributes and telesmatics, in 1855. Eliphas Levi, the pseudonymous goyish magus, wrote as follows in his *Doctrine and Ritual of Transcendental Magic*:

> *Yes, we confront here that phantom of all terrors, the dragon of all theogonies, the Ahriman of the Persians, the Typhon of the Egyptians, the Python of the Greeks, the old serpent of the Hebrews, the fantastic monster, the nightmare, the Croquemitaine, the gargoyle, the great beast of the Middle Ages, and—worse than all these—the Baphomet of the Templars, the bearded idol of the alchemist, the obscene deity of Mendes, the goat of the Sabbath...the exact figure of the terrible emperor of night, with all his attributes and all his characters... a chimera, a malformed sphinx, a synthesis of deformities.*

Let me ask you something. Does this extensive roll call of bugaboos and boogymen seem to be missing someone—and a really big someone at that? Take a look at the particulars, made definitively manifest in Eliphas Levi's frontispiece engraving. We see a goat's head, its horns, floppy ears and beard forming a pentagram, planted on a single point (recently vulgarized by the Republicans). We see wings, a woman's breasts, a caduceus standing in for the hermaphroditical ithyphallus, and the delicately lascivious hands of an archbishop flipping the two-fingered benediction salute.

You know exactly who this is, even though his horrendous name escapes mention. In fact, from the standpoint of a certain widespread orthodoxy, his dread moniker should subsume the entire list. It should appear at the top of the paragraph, with all the other names merely appended as AKAs. And why does this unspecified monster merit such puffing up?

Well, consider the formidable nature of his opposite number, the monstrous hypertrophism of his arch-nemesis, Superman to his Lex Luthor, Batman to his irritating little prick with smeared makeup. Our unnamed spook goes up against the greatest monster of all: *Gaw-w-w-wd*, with a capital *Gee* and a really impressive *whizz*. To serve as the all-but-equally-matched sparring partner of such a Supreme Being, you need to have *The Absolute Eternal Principle of Evil* sequined across your spandex stretchy pants. Satan himself is a smashing novelty act. So, why would one of Europe's greatest occultists disdain to mention him?

An unprecedented kind of mind has suddenly appeared out of nowhere during the last couple millennia. In human history's long context, this mental mutant is more grotesque than Abigail and Brittany Hensel rolled into one. It is characterized by a megalomaniacal sense of itself. Enflamed and encrusted with growths like the insupportable noggin of the Elephant

Man, this *self* cannot help but look upon the world to presuppose a slightly larger Self: the One and Only CEO and Sole Manufacturer of Absolutely Everything.

When first confronted by this bizarre pathology, the poor Romans are said to have been so flustered as to react self-defensively, with large carnivores. In the present book, if you peer deep into the illustrations and carefully read between the lines of Canto Three, you might meet one of the Empire's top wranglers, Carpophorus the *bestiarius*, who taught lions (and, even more effectively, mastiffs) to exterminate some of the earliest vectors of the *Gaw-w-w-wd* bacterium. A couple of cantos later, if you peruse our pages with no less attentiveness, you might be able to say *wie gehts* to the matron of Buchenwald, *Oberaufseherin* Ilse Koch, who helped quarantine some descendants of the folks responsible for incubating the original strain.

These days, with modernity's benumbed metaphysical instincts, *Gaw-w-w-wd* is sometimes seen merely as a vaporous joke. Dawkins and dead Hitchens are all over YouTube, setting forth the only two alternatives discussable in contemporary major industrialized cosmology. On the one hand, they fearlessly inform us, there is a spiritual vacuum more nearly perfect than that of deep space, as it contains no dark matter. (The smart money's on that one.) On the other hand, we have this burlesque of a Popish Heavenly Father-cum-Prot Lord, as kidnapped from his Jewish tribal tent.

The Aghori mendicant tiptoeing among cremations on the Ganges bank; the Uncompahgre squaw waltzing in mescalinical bliss through the Utah tar sand; the Theosophist humming ragas on a Pasadena bus bench; the Osaka salary-man sardined on a commuter train: all of these honest heathens would jeer at Dawkins and dead Hitchens, and dismiss their dialectic as counterintuitive on the one hand, infantile on the other. And so would Eliphas Levi himself, being consciously versed in the Once Universal *Prisca Theologia*.

"Spiritual vacuum," did those neo-atheists say? In all times and places, right up until Descartes had his triple nocturnal emission during that long weekend on the Donau, just about everyone knew *the air is full of spirits*, as Philo Judaeus said. And not only the air. The dirt and rocks, the water and fire, everything positively pullulates with centers of consciousness, a goodly proportion of whom would appear monstrous to the uninitiated eye. There seems to be a scarcely imaginable number of varieties and ranks and orders—

*...our Gnomes, our Undines, Salamanders, Sylphs,
our Elementals and their mighty ilk...*

—you name it. *Kobolds*, even. The unseen universe resembles nothing so much as a gander down a microscope at a quantity of pond scum, or maybe one of those promotional scuba diving videos which the Hashemite Kingdom of Jordan's Tourism Ministry shoots at the Gulf of Aqaba. Amoebas, sea slugs, winged gryphons are everywhere.

As far as Jehovah goes, our tiptoeing Hindu, our Amerind peyotist, our gentle Theosophizer, our son of Shinto God Hirohito, our French occultist—not a single member of our lovely pagan quintet would scoff like a neo-atheist at the notion of that big bully's *existence*. (That's the key word to keep in mind.) They're happy to have YHWH out there, and gladly include him among Philo Judaeus' unseen beings. He's just the most obnoxious, the biggest oaf with the worst B.O., the Dubya-Obama of the clan. Miguel Serrano, prophet-seer-revelator of Esoteric Hitlerism, calls him *The Plagiarist Demiurge*. According to the Valentinians, he is a *monster spawned by Sophia*. Boastful, blind and insane, he's the Unitary Executive, the jealous god ("I'm the decider"), and thou shalt have no others before Dubyadabaoth-Ialdaobama.

Speaking of other "gods," it's high time for a non-monster to appear—rather, *not* to appear. Listen now to Xenophanes of Colophon:

*One god there is, in no way like mortal creatures in bodily form
or in the thought of his mind. The whole of him thinks, the whole
of him hears. He stays always motionless in the same place. It is
not fitting that he should move about now this way, now that...
Effortlessly he wields all things by the thought of his mind.*

In Christendom and thereabouts, this immobile, bodiless Mind is routinely confused or morphed with *Gaw-w-w-wd*. But you can't have monstrosity without deformity, and there's no deformity without attributes. And what is Satan's rival but a bundle of attributes every bit as lumpy as Croquemitaine's?

When you come close as humanly possible to glimpsing Xenophanes' motionless "god"; when you've gotten the barest hint of the Theosophical *Akasha*, or Pure Spirit; when through your brain briefly flits the most delicately adumbrated semi-notion of what the Hindus call *That*—you can't help but be stunned by the outrageousness of the monotheist's blasphemy. You begin to understand the rationale behind certain exhibitions in the Roman arena.

Far from constituting the impossible combination of personal god and ultimate reality, the monotheistic deity is nothing more than the jerry-rigger of existence—a botched job by definition: both Frankenstein and Frankenstein's fuck-up. What unspeakable presumption to tart up the Creator Monster and try to fob him off as the Ultimate Reality! Plunging the unthinkable *That* elbow-deep in AIDS babies, Sub-Saharan famines, genocidal wars and all those other theodicial migraines that sometimes cause thoughtful priests to suffer erectile dysfunction right in the middle of an altar boy—it boils down to a congenital deficiency, or retardation, of the imagination peculiar to the sons of Shem and the cults they spawned.

If something has hands that can get besmirched in the work of creation, it can be named. And if it can be named, or even imagined, it exists, every bit as materially as you and I. It will rot eventually, like the little arms and legs skinned and pickled and fricasseed by *Oberaufseherin* Ilse Koch, who camouflages her climacteric bloat between these pages.

To those who know how to read the New Testament narratives correctly (*i.e.*, the same way *We'll See Who Seduces Whom* should be read: between the lines, as a veiled esoteric text), it comes as no surprise when the nineteenth verse of the second chapter of the Beloved Disciple's gospel states—

Thou believest that there is one God; thou dost well: the devils also believe, and tremble.

The correct interpretation of this passage is as follows: *we* the clued-in, as opposed to *thee*, are nowhere near as superstitious as the contemptible devils, including those demonic grotesqueries behind the pulpit, who "believe, and tremble," and lurk and leer and spasm in their silken chasubles with the boner teepee in the middle.

Of course, Baphomet himself, *AKA* Aleister Crowley, says it even better than Saint John:

…the vulgarians conceive of nothing beyond the Creator.

So, open our book and let vulgar *Gaw-w-w-wd* in. He'll be the bitch of your personal Buchenwald who flays and pickles and fricassees your babies:

he'll be the *bestiarius* who goads the ox that butt-rapes you to death in the Coliseum. Let him be the biggest monster trundling down our colorful road. *Gaw-w-w-wd* is the three-hundred-pound drooler on the bus, seated right across the aisle from you, the one with the erect phallus and the guns and knives bristling from his greasy raincoat pockets.

Stay calm. Don't look at him. Pretend he's not there. You don't want him noticing you. Stare straight down at our book in your lap and wait to disembark calmly, but with all available dispatch, at the next stop. For god's sake, whatever you do, don't lay this lovely volume aside and fish out a grimoire from your backpack and start intoning barbarous syllables of invocation. Don't call out the aliases of his rival. That *Doctrine and Ritual of Transcendental Magic* only encourages Heavenly *Faw-w-w-w-wther*. It makes him think you take him seriously.

And, this freak mutant, this botched late-term abortion, is not, under any circumstances, to be taken seriously. You must never doubt that *Gaw-w-w-wd* wields a certain percentage of the omnipresent, omniscient omnipotence of the Supreme Being he wants you to think he is. And, compared to us, he comes a lot closer to the timelessness that his priests claim for him, and also extend to his "Eternal Foe," in the name of public relations. But, what, in the end, do those perfectly mensurable superiorities signify?

Serrano's "plagiarist Demiurge" may have mucked us together like golems from the mud, and set us squirming and sinning elbow-to-elbow with all the bugaboos and boogymen that you will find among the words and images in this book. But he did not insufflate our lungs; neither did he gastrulate our astral monads. We, the victims and beneficiaries of this strange material dispensation, are his brats and his bottom bitches, but not his feats of legerdemain. We owe him nothing but lower back pain, post-nasal drip, dandruff, and so forth.

On the far side of the Khyber Pass, learned Brahmans who have memorized the Vedas can, on a whim, with a single thought, annihilate the entire universe, including all of its most elaborately tricked-out and puffed-up monster-gods.

Meanwhile, our own cheap imitation Brahmans, Dawkins and dead Hitchens, are sounding like a couple of seven-year-old lads. They're tucked nervously in their bunk bed for the night. Dawkins is averring loudly that *Oberaufseherin* Ilse Koch is not really hiding in the closet, waiting for the light to be turned off, her sharp flaying knife at the ready. Our bedtime boys bravely announce to the darkness that Carpophorus the *bestiarius* by no means lurks at Frau Ilse's side. His favorite rutting elephant is most definitely *not* straining at the leash, sniffing dead Hitchens' sneakers with its lubed-up proboscis.

Just keep talking, boys. Don't worry about a thing.